Ox 6 41

PLAINSONG
ACCOMPANIMENT

PLAINSONG ACCOMPANIMENT

By J. H. ARNOLD

WITH A PREFACE BY GEOFFREY SHAW

OXFORD UNIVERSITY PRESS
LONDON · HUMPHREY MILFORD

1927

PRINTED IN ENGLAND BY
HENDERSON & SPALDING LTD
SYLVAN GROVE
CAMBERWELL
LONDON
S E
15

DEDICATED
in gratitude
to the Church which is at
ST MARY THE VIRGIN
PRIMROSE HILL

ACKNOWLEDGEMENTS

The Author is glad to record his first debt of gratitude to Mr Geoffrey Shaw for the constant encouragement and the valuable advice which he has given while this book has been in preparation, and for his permission to include the accompaniments of two Glorias. It is a pleasure also to thank his old master Mr Martin Shaw for an accompaniment of a Kyrie. The late Rev. Dr Palmer's services to the Church in the cause of Plainsong are well known, and the Author wishes to acknowledge his own share of indebtedness; in particular for the permission which Dr Palmer had given for his transcriptions to be drawn upon in illustrating the text of this book. Acknowledgements are also due to the Plainsong and Mediaeval Music Society, and to St Mary's Convent, Wantage, for permission to draw similarly upon their service books; and to Mr. C. J. Revell for his able help in reading proofs.

My dear Jack,

For several reasons I do not find it easy to write a Preface to your book. *Imprimis*, a formal preface by me may give your public the impression that I know all there is to be known of Plainsong, from which high eminence I deign to bless your book. So far is this from the truth that I hasten now to place myself in the humbler ranks of those who have no shame in confessing that they know but one thing of Plainsong: they love it.

Secondo, I have watched with ever-increasing interest the growth of your book. I have sat late with the thrill of triumph when some recondite authority has confirmed your view; I have gone to bed indignant at his failure to see eye to eye with you. In short, I have been so near the book all the time that my blessing can have no positive or critical value. It must have a value relative to my partiality for, and indeed my faith in, the book.

Terzio, you and I, as fellow workers at St Mary's, share together a privilege so lovely that we cannot imagine that the bond between us could ever be broken. We have grown to think alike in our work. (Though I own I have not yet grown to the measure of your strong principle and considered judgement in the matter of the right place for my organ music, nor even, alas, for the key of the cupboard in which I ought to put it away.) There are many who know this, and they may with justice question the wisdom of a Swan prefacing a work by an Edgar. ' This preface to Edgar's book ', such an one might say, ' would come better from Dickins, with maybe a footnote or two from Jones.'

All things considered, I feel happier in writing you this letter of good-will. If honest work, careful searching, exact scholarship, and steady enthusiasm count at all in the scale of human judgement, your book should be widely accepted.

I think the book's strong point is its attempt to reduce to order and system the many scattered fragments of musical theory and practice relevant to its subject. I also greatly like the numerous examples you give. These should be of real value not only to students, but also to the many who are on the look-out for suitable accompaniments to Psalm Tones, Hymn Melodies, Mass Music, etc.

I believe there is no branch of practical musicianship more fascinating than Plainsong Accompaniment, and certainly no branch more neglected. I should always advise those who have anything to do with setting words to music to study Plainsong Accompaniment carefully. As it is, many a good song does not ' go ' well because the composer cannot bring nuance into his accompaniment.

If I write more I shall defeat my object. My letter will have become a Preface.

Yours,

GEOFFREY SHAW

All Saints' Day 1926

CONTENTS

INTRODUCTION

The revival of plainsong in the English Church may be considered to date from about 1841, by which year the Gregorian psalm-tones had been brought into use at St Peter's-in-the-East, Oxford, and in Lichfield Cathedral. In each case, however, the adaptation had been a matter of local contrivance, and it was not until 1843 that any printed choir-book became available for a wider public. In that year William Dyce issued his stately *Order of Daily Service, the Litany, and Order of Holy Communion, with Plain-Tune*, which was a careful adaptation of Merbecke's *Book of Common Prayer Noted*; and about the same time Richard Redhead, the organist of Margaret Chapel, now All Saints, Margaret Street, published his ' *Laudes Diurnae*, The Psalter and Canticles set and pointed to Gregorian Tones, with a preface on Antiphonal Chanting by Rev. Frederick Oakeley '. From thence onwards the story of the revival has been one of steady development in the face of heavy odds—fanatical prejudice without, uninformed enthusiasm within, misrepresentation, false models at hand for reference, and the peculiar musical and theological inheritances of the Victorian age to distort perspective. But the growth of half a century had been sturdy, and when the results of many years' patient research by the Benedictines of Solesmes were shown to the world, new impulse was given to desires that were already strong, and new life and light began to stream into the movement which has never since paused in its progress.

To-day the old prejudices are all but broken down. The days are past when musicians can speak of plainsong as a barbarity. These timeless melodies are undoubtedly becoming more widely known and better loved. There is on all hands a glad recognition that here lies the solution of some of the weariest of our church music problems, and there is a frank admission of the peculiar fitness of plainsong for clothing liturgical forms. Its exponents are numerous, weighty, and persuasive. Their arguments are unanswerable. Texts are available in many forms and explanatory literature is abundant and, on the whole, inexpensive. Living examples are becoming more numerous, and ably conducted demonstrations and lectures are increasingly common. It is welcomed and blessed by the Archbishops' Committee on Music in Worship. In fact, the battle is won. Yet the progress lags.

The Vicar is convinced, and his assistant is open-minded. Moreover, he is in the habit of taking his congregation into his confidence, and he carries his Church Council with him. His knowledge of his subject is sufficient to equip him for teaching others to sing, and his enthusiasm is infectious. His choirmen are churchmen, and they are humble. His organist is a young amateur who is glad to learn, and is sufficiently keen about his work to have become a member of the Church Music Society, but his practical acquaintance with plainsong can be measured by a couple of Sundays at Cowley and a Gregorian Festival at St Paul's. It is precisely at this point that the halt has to be called, and although the right material may be at hand, unless the constructive ability is forthcoming, the chasm is likely to remain unbridged. This unquestionably is the experience of many a church where all may be ready for an introduction of plainsong into its services, but with the best dispositions in the world the organist cannot provide an adequate accompaniment, not because it is difficult to play, but because he does not know what to play. Essentially his problem is to learn an unknown language.

It is not really difficult—in fact, the rules are surprisingly few—but if he is to come to grips with his subject, definite instruction must be obtained. It is true he may find ready-made assistance, some of it excellent, in the various harmonies which have been published for the accompaniment of masses, and he will doubtless take stock of the suggested harmonies for the office hymns in his hymnal, but for obvious reasons the accompaniment of psalmody is barely touched in this manner, and he will quickly realize the importance of becoming entirely self-reliant in all these directions if he aims at handling his subject in a craftsmanlike way.

Without doubt his ideal course will be to put himself under the instruction of one who is a master in the art of accompanying plainsong, and to worship in a church where he may soak in it, but as this counsel of perfection is beyond the reach of most, he will perforce have to depend entirely upon text books and published examples. It is with the object of helping to bridge this gap that the following pages have been put forth. Evidently they are not addressed to those who already know their art, but rather to the novice whose musical education is slender. The aim has been to take nothing for granted beyond a very elementary knowledge of harmony, covering the use of the common chord and its inversions. This at least is necessary as a foundation, and if it has not already been acquired, the student had better set to work on mastering, say, the first six chapters of Stainer's *Harmony* (Novello) or of Macpherson's *Practical Harmony* (Joseph Williams), or Part I of Kitson's *Elementary Harmony* (Clarendon Press), and he should have broken this ground well by the time he reaches the fourth chapter of the present volume.

For choir books to work with for exercise purposes, he is directed to those which have been drawn on for all the examples which follow; viz.

The Sarum Psalter, Rev. Dr Palmer (St Mary's Convent, Wantage) *or A Manual of Plainsong*, Briggs & Frere (Novello, Wardour Street, London, W.1)

The Ordinary of the Mass[1] (Plainsong & Mediaeval Music Society, Nashdom Abbey, Burnham, Bucks)

---

[1] The Plainsong & Mediaeval Music Society publishes a selection of the masses contained in the *Ordinary* in a cheap reprint entitled *The Plainsong of the Holy Communion*. (7d.)

English Hymnal (Oxford University Press, London)
Introits (St Mary's Convent, Wantage)
Additional Settings of Certain Canticles (St Mary's Convent, Wantage)

Much valuable explanatory matter will be found in
Elements of Plainsong (Plainsong & Mediaeval Music Society)
The Teaching and Accompaniment of Plainsong, Burgess (Novello)

It is hoped that it may not be outside the rightful scope of this book to draw special attention to
Music in Worship, Report of the Archbishops' Committee (S.P.C.K.)
The Complete Organist, by Harvey Grace (Grant Richards, St Martin's Street, London W.)
Church Music, by A. S. Duncan-Jones (Robert Scott, Paternoster Row, London, E.C. 4)

which, beyond having a very direct bearing on the subject in hand, are deep wells of stimulating and broadening information where the embryo Church musician may drink deeply.

CHAPTER I

NOTATION

UNISONOUS NATURE.

The student has discovered, it is assumed, that all plainsong is unisonous; that is to say, whether it be psalm-tone, hymn, antiphon,
versicle, creed, sursum corda, sanctus, amen, or whatever form it may
take, it consists of a melody only, which is sung by all voices at the same
pitch or an octave apart. It is possible to decorate this melody by harmonic accompaniment, either instrumental or vocal, but it must be
quite clearly remembered that the chant is perfectly complete as it
stands, and those who have heard the plainchant adequately sung in its
bare beauty without the use of the organ will perhaps have recognized
that, far from requiring any harmonic assistance, the freely moving
melody sung by one or two voices, or all voices in unison, may actually
suffer by any addition. It certainly will do so if the accompaniment is
ill devised. The purist will maintain that the best accompaniment in
the world will in some measure detract from the beauty of the plainchant, and theoretically he cannot be denied, but the organ as an
accompanying instrument has come to stay, and as the following pages
are designed to help forward an intelligent use of it to that end, it is
not here intended to labour the contention. By realizing the position,
however, the beginner will approach his subject humbly, and in the
days of his proficiency he will be led, it is hoped, to ensure that regular
opportunities are given to his congregation of hearing the plainchant
unadorned. He may seek to do this particularly in Lent and Passiontide.
Incidentally, his choir will reap no small advantage.

NOTATION.

It cannot be too strongly urged that the only door through which the
organist can attain to any degree of excellence in his accompaniment of
plainsong is a vocal one, and from the first he must learn to sing the
melodies and, furthermore, sing them from their own traditional
notation. This course is essential, as by it alone can the right rhythm
of the chant be really captured.

The notation is no doubt the first and most striking of the un-
familiarities with which the student of plainsong is confronted, and his
first acquaintance with a page entirely composed of the traditional stave
(e.g., English Hymnal, p. 882) will convey an impression of mystery.
Of mystery, however, there is none, nor any difficulties which cannot
be mastered by a couple of hours' study.

Historically, the form may be described as the earliest full-fledged
development of staff notation, the direct ancestor of our modern forms,

B

and the outcome of an earlier system of neums or signs which served the purpose of memory-prompters for melodies already familiar. These neums were capable of indicating niceties of rhythm, but were insufficient in themselves to record the exact pitch of each note. The addition of a staff, however—at first a single line—had the twofold effect of defining the pitch-relation of successive notes, and (by the time the four-line staff had been definitely established in the eleventh century) of more or less crystallizing the shapes of the notes into something almost identical with what are used now for the same purpose.

This notation has been retained, not only because it is traditional, but because it exactly fits its purpose; it has no essential difficulties and allows the groups of notes to show their own rhythm as no transcription into modern notation, with its suggestions of exact time values, can.

Further, or perhaps consequently, the old notation has a certain quality which is akin to the symbolism of shorthand, in that it is very often easy to read a whole group of notes at a single glance, while a corresponding row of quavers will require, in their exact similarity, something more like spelling out.

The type of notation as printed to-day is highly picturesque, but as practised by the mediaeval scribe it affords instances of extreme beauty lavished over the pages of the old choir books of the later middle ages. Magnificent examples are easy of access in the British Museum, the Victoria and Albert Museum, and elsewhere, and the student will do well to make some opportunities of examining these at first hand. He will be rewarded if there springs up in him some feeling of affection for these venerable forms amongst which it will become his pleasure to move about at ease.

It will now be convenient to consider the peculiarities of the square notation.

(*a*) The stave consists of four lines only. This is generally sufficient for holding the comparatively restricted compass of most melodies without any recourse to ledger lines. These, however, are freely used if necessary by modern printers and they are more convenient than the older method, which was to raise or lower the clef for that portion of the melody which could not be held by the stave. As lines of notes and text were closely packed in the old service books, partly perhaps for reasons of economy, the change of clef would be natural, and as this method is still commonly used, the student should familiarize himself with it. It presents no real difficulty, the relative pitch of the note immediately following the change of clef being indicated by a 'guide'

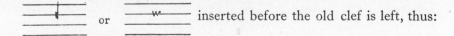 inserted before the old clef is left, thus:

So may we, by God pro-mo-ted, share that heaven which ye pos-sess

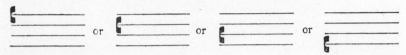

This convenient guide is also usually placed at the end of each line of music as a forerunner of the first note on the next stave

(*b*) The clefs most commonly used are the C clef:

(the marked line bears the note C, other notes following accordingly); and the F clef:

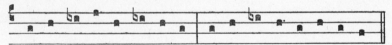

the marked line bearing F similarly.

Occasionally the flat (♭) is used as a clef sign, thus indicating that all the notes which fall in the space so marked are B flat. It may be here remarked that the only accidental used in plainsong is the flattening of the B, the use of the flat sign (♭) always implying B flat. Otherwise, so far as the notation is concerned, the diatonic scale is strictly adhered to. The flat sign is most frequently employed immediately before the particular B which it is intended to flatten,

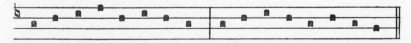

and is effective for that occurrence of the note only. Less commonly, however, when it is used as a clef sign, it is effective so long as the clef remains unchanged. For instance, the above example might equally well have been written thus :

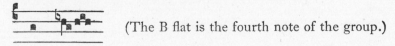

When a flattened B occurs in the middle of a group of notes, the sign usually precedes the group, not the note, e.g.:

(The B flat is the fourth note of the group.)

(c) The spacing of notes or group of notes on the stave has reference to the syllables to which the notes are allied, i.e., if a phrase consists of eight syllables, the corresponding notes will be spaced out into eight notes or note-groups as the case may be.

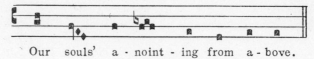

Our souls' a - noint - ing from a - bove.

A group of two or more notes allied to one syllable is termed a neum.

(d) The 'bar lines' commonly used do not mark equal divisions of time as in modern music, but the division of the text into phrases by means of pauses which vary in degree according to the nature of the bar.

The full division bar[1] implies a full breath and a rallentando of the note or notes immediately preceding it.

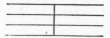

The half bar implies a shorter breath and a slighter rallentando; and a still slighter break is indicated in some editions by a quarter bar.

The final division bar (the double bar) quite naturally implies a marked rallentando, and requires no further explanation.

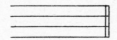

It should be noted, however, that the double bar may also be used to sub-divide the whole text into main sections, and thus employed it indicates the alternation of voices.[2] It may also show how far the chanters are to precent, though in many editions an asterisk in the text is substituted:

O praise the Lord, all ye his An-gels : ex - cel-ling in... &c.,

[1] To avoid the possibility of confusion, the word 'division' will be used to indicate the portion of music which lies between two consecutive 'division bars'.

[2] Creed and *Gloria in excelsis* thus sub-divided, however, are commonly sung full throughout.

_ O praise the Lord,[*] all ye his An-gels : ex - cel -ling in... &c.,

(*e*) Whereas in modern notes diversities in shape indicate corresponding diversities in time value, the various shapes of the square notation have no such significance. The unit is the *punctum* ▪ (a single horizontal stroke of a broad quill held sideways), and all other notes are merely variations of this, developed from the earlier neumatic signs and fashioned largely by conditions of penmanship. For instance, to indicate a little descending scale, it would be natural for the scribe merely to turn his broad pen and draw it down diagonally, hence the familiar diamond notes ◆◆. The basic principle is that all the notes have equal time value. The unit may appear also as a *virga* ▪ or ▪, but once again no difference in time value is indicated by the stem. Originally, no doubt, the stem of the *virga* (as the name suggests) was the essence of the note, indicating a rise in pitch, a higher note. It may be observed that the *virga* never stands alone now, and that it is only by exception that its stem or 'verge' does not point down towards the next note following. No peculiar execution is demanded.

(*f*) The notes and their typical combinations (neums), together with a transcription into modern notation, follow:—

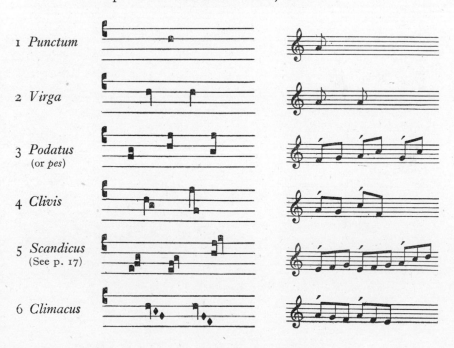

1 *Punctum*

2 *Virga*

3 *Podatus*
   (or *pes*)

4 *Clivis*

5 *Scandicus*
   (See p. 17)

6 *Climacus*

7 *Torculus*

8 *Porrectus*

(Here the thick, oblique stroke merely indicates two notes, one at the line or space at which the stroke begins, and one at the end.)

The first note of every neum receives a vocal stress or accent, as indicated in the transcriptions above. This is a cardinal rule which cannot be grasped too soon. Further instruction on the accentuation of neums has been delayed until Chapter II on Rhythm.

Some of the above neums are liable to have their last note curtailed, and they are printed accordingly in order to indicate a specially light treatment, e.g.:

This half note occurs only at the end of a syllable when, in the act of passing from one syllable to another, there is necessarily a natural merging or absorption of sound caused, for instance, by the juxtaposition of two such consonants as *n* and *d*.

sus - tain - er   de - fen - der   save   me

It is the accompanist's business, of course, to understand these liquescent forms, though his accompaniment will hardly be affected by them.

Neums composed either of extensions or combinations of those set out in the table above are very common. For instance:—

The structure of the last two examples clearly shews them to consist of combinations of two distinct simple neums rather than extensions or developments of a simple form. They are therefore known as

' compound neums', and the distinction will be important to remember when accentuation is considered in the next chapter.

Two additional forms may be noted:—

9 *Strophicus*  Sung as two or three tied notes, except that in the latter case (the *tristropha*) the voices may interpret the centre note as a very light undulation down (perhaps a quarter tone). The accompanist treats it as three tied notes.

10 *Quilisma*  Usually in the centre of three ascending notes, it is weak itself, and strengthens the note which precedes it, thus:

It is not necessary to learn the names of the neums in order to sing or accompany them.

READING FROM PLAINSONG NOTATION.

The function of the C or F of the clef is not to indicate pitch, but to determine the relationship of the notes to each other. For instance,

but if the student will settle in his mind on one or the other, and has mastered the forms of the neums set out above, he already knows that he is concerned with the white notes only, and will find no difficulty in playing any simple melody direct from the old notation. It will form a useful preliminary exercise for him to play from the square notation (without transposition) the melodies of the following hymns in the *English Hymnal*:

736, 1, 2, 95, 165, 735, 51, 18, 141, 737.

It will have been noticed that in several of the above examples the tunes as they stand are set at an inconvenient pitch, e.g., No. 95, line 2:

is far too high, and the tune will have to be transposed to suit the pitch of the voices, to something like this:

This sort of transposition is most frequently needed and undoubtedly presents a difficulty in the accompaniment of plainsong. However, where the melodies are well known (especially in the psalm tones) this will be no stumbling block, and as in his student days the organist will be at pains to write out his own accompaniments for the less simple forms, the difficulty will be merely initial.

A quick method of reading an unfamiliar melody is to imagine a fifth line on the top of the four-line stave, and to think of the square notes as being modern notation.[1] A key signature will, of course, have to be imagined, which will vary according to whether the 𝄡 is on the 'D' or 'B' or 'G' line, and so on. Thus:—

---

[1] This method of approach is anticipated by some continental editions of the Latin text (notably those from the Librairie St.-Grégoire at Grenoble), which place the traditional notes on a five-line stave with an equivalent of the modern key signature; for instance—

vós óm-nes,* qui transí- tis per ví-

am,   atténdi-te, et vidé- te,

In the more strictly traditional manner, this would open—

&c.

A weakness of the method is that if the clef changes in the course of the melody, the thought of the modern parallel must be dropped. However, as there will be a guide before the change to indicate the next note, and as the tonality will have been well established in the mind, the difficulty is not great.

Students, however, who are familiar with the tonic solfa system will find no great difficulty in transposition.

TRANSCRIPTION.

Various note-units have been employed for transcribing plainsong into modern notation. None is entirely satisfactory. The use of the quaver has now become almost general, largely because it rightly suggests a lighter, quicker movement than the leisurely minim, and also because neums are easily indicated by the tied quavers. It has also become common to indicate rallentandos at the end of phrases by the use of the crotchet. However, the juxtaposition of quaver and crotchet cannot fail to suggest rigid time values in the modern sense, and throughout these pages it has been preferred to adhere to the exclusive use of the quaver, except for a reciting note, which is usually represented by a minim.

CHAPTER II

RHYTHM

Of the many definitions of rhythm which have been attempted, it is the exception which does not express the idea of regularity, and in the minds of those who are responsible for the music in our parish churches, the word would almost inevitably suggest something like ' four in a bar '. The student who has considered the peculiarities of the plainchant notation in the previous chapter has already discovered that

    (*a*) bars, in the modern sense, do not exist in Gregorian music, and

    (*b*) all notes have an equal time value.

In what, then, does the rhythm of plainsong consist? Firstly, the chant derives its rhythm from the words which it clothes, and where it is syllabic (i.e., where it consists of one note per syllable) it does so exclusively. On this too much emphasis cannot be laid. The pulse of the words will be the plainsong student's first and last concern, and the sooner he can disentangle his conception of ' rhythm ' from the idea of mechanical regularity in recurrence of accent, the better will he approach the right interpretation of the rich and varied rhythm of the music with which he will be dealing. The following comparison with a measured example will serve as an illustration:

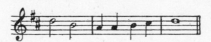

presents a very definite rhythm, essentially independent of words, whereas:

means nothing as it stands, because it possesses no rhythm of its own. Clothe it with words, however:

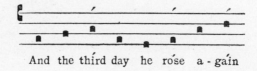

And the third day he rose a - gain

and it has become instinct with life, because it has taken to itself the rhythm of the words—an irregular rhythm in this case, be it marked. Or give it other words, and it takes a different rhythm:

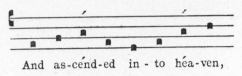

And as-cénd-ed in - to héa-ven,

Or yet again:

Who for us mén and for...

The rhythm of the plainsong, then, is the rhythm of the words, and whether the pulse be regular or irregular, so it will be reflected in, or shine through, the music.

From the fact that with the exception of the office hymns, the liturgical text is wholly prose, and therefore in an irregular rhythm, it is evident that the vast bulk of plainsong must present an irregular rhythm correspondingly. It is this freedom from the bondage of the regularly recurring accent which gives plainchant its flexibility, and makes it peculiarly suitable for the prose of psalms, canticles, and mass, and at the same time marks it off as a thing apart from any other type of music.

The manner in which the plainchant takes the rhythm of the words is precisely the manner in which the words deliver their rhythm, that is, by enunciating certain syllables with a stronger emphasis than others.

For example, if the sentence: ' And the third day he rose again according to the Scriptures ', be enunciated according to the principles of good reading, it will be observed that a stress is laid upon the syllable ' third ' ' rose ', ' -cord- ', ' Scrip-', with perhaps a lighter stress on '-gain '. But it is an emphasis of stress, or weight, or pressing, not of lengthening the time-value, which contrasts these syllables with their neighbours, and it is precisely this method which must be applied when singing the words.

It will further be observed that, carefully yet naturally enunciated, all the syllables have *practically* an equal time-value, and it is just that degree of equality which is intended when we speak of all notes in plainchant as having an equal time-value. In the course of natural speech, it is obvious that the word ' strength ' will take a slightly longer time to pronounce than the word ' with ', but if the natural enunciation is good, the time relationship of the two words will certainly be nearer a pair of quavers than a dotted quaver and a semiquaver. The rhythm then of ' strength with his arm ' will be better indicated by ♪ ♪ ♪ ♪

than by 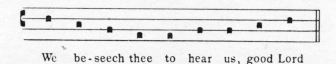, which is exactly that mechanical type of rhythm which is the very antithesis of *cantus planus*.

It may now be better appreciated why no transcription into modern notation is really satisfactory. No form of it can avoid suggesting rigid time-values. This matter of word-rhythm is at the very root of the study of plainchant. It is the breath of life for chanter and organist alike, and at the risk of repetition, a further example will be quoted:

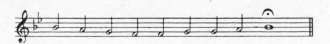

We   be - seech thee   to   hear   us, good Lord

Not so many years ago, this fragment would hardly have escaped transcription, thus:—

with the obvious ponderous results. The natural accentuation gives three strong syllables, which will be 'pressed', not lengthened, thus:—

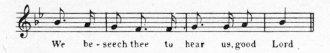

We   be - seech thee   to   hear   us,   good Lord

The improper lengthening of the strong syllables, combined with a corresponding clipping of the weak ones, leads to something like this:

We   be - seech thee   to   hear   us, good   Lord

The prescription, then, for the treatment of the strong syllable would seem to be ' press lightly, but do not stay '. Attention must be directed to keeping the other syllables light and even.

So far we have considered only syllabic plainsong. Directly we come into touch with a more ornate form embracing neums, a fresh element is introduced inasmuch as the music, qua music, will have a contribution of its own to make to the rhythm. The first note of every neum is a strong note, i.e., it is sung with a slight stress. It must be clearly understood that this in no way disturbs the principles already accepted, but is something additional from outside. If a syllable is strong in natural speech, it will be strong musically in all circumstances. The stress of the first note of a neum is additional, and is made irrespective of whether the syllable to which the neum is allied be strong or weak. We shall therefore have to consider the possibility of both a verbal accent and a musical accent.

In the original example: ' And the third day he rose again according to the Scriptures ', it was seen that there were five syllables which could be called strong. Were the traditional melody for this phrase entirely syllabic (which it is not), five strong notes would be implied, in this manner:

And the third day he rose a - gain   ac-córd-ing to the Scriptures.

However, the melody actually embodies one neum, which happens to be allied to a verbally weak syllable ' ac- '. Therefore, by virtue of its alliance with a neum, the weak ' ac- ' acquires a stress at its first note, and the number of stressed notes becomes six:

And the third day he rose a - gain   ac-córd-ing to the Scriptures.

The neum might quite well have been allied to a verbally strong syllable, in which case, by the law of simple addition, the already strong syllable would acquire a slightly additional strength for its first note; so the first note of a neum will, strictly speaking, be stressed proportionately with the strength of the allied syllable. If that syllable is weak, the stress will be very slight, but it will be there. The salient point for the student to grasp clearly is that, in all circumstances, a stress is to be given to every verbally strong syllable, and to the first note of every neum.

Within any given neum, then, the initial accentuation is clear. But from the inability of more than three consecutive musical notes to express themselves rhythmically without the aid of a second accent, there follows the fact that in neums consisting of four notes or more, there must be some secondary accent. The existence and position of this are important, but it must be remembered that no such secondary stress is as strongly marked even as the slight stress at the opening of the neum. It is aptly referred to sometimes as the ' rhythmic touch ', being only just sufficient to define whether a group of five notes, for instance, falls into a 2+3 rhythm or 3+2. In fact, it is hardly an exaggeration to say that the stress is mental rather than vocal. Nearly always it occurs at the third note of the group; thus, normally[1], it is characteristic of all four-note simple neums to fall into 2+2, and five-note neums into 2+3; for example:—

Two types of five-note neum, however (the *pessubpunctis* and the *pessubpunctis resupinus*), generally receive the rhythmic touch at the fourth note instead, for instance:—

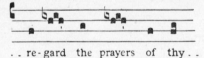

---

[1] Although the above examples may be regarded as typical and normal, the position of a secondary stress in a given neum is not fixed unchangeably, as neums are not separable from their context. The ultimate key to the position of such secondary stresses lies in the universal law by which all rhythm (musical or verbal) must fall into fractional units of either two or three notes or syllables each, *i.e.* binary or ternary feet. Arising out of this the following circumstances should be observed:—

(i) A single note allied to a weak syllable and immediately following a neum, is reckoned rhythmically with that neum. Consequently—there being no such thing as a 4-note unit—although a 3-note neum as such has no secondary stress, it will necessarily acquire one if followed by a single weak note; thus

.. re-gard the prayers of thy..

(*A secondary stress is marked by a small perpendicular stroke below.*)

Immediately before a division bar, however, a single note, being a lengthened note (see pp. 18, 37), is counted for this purpose as if it were a strong note, irrespective of whether the allied syllable is strong or weak, and the last note of a neum preceding it will not receive a secondary stress; hence

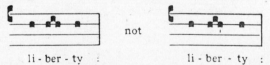

not

li - ber - ty :   li - ber - ty :

(ii) A weak single note following a simple four-note neum draws the secondary stress from its normal position at the third note to the fourth; thus

Int Christmas

.. shall   be   up - on ..

(iii) The final note of any neum which immediately precedes a division bar or pause, being a lengthened note, is counted rhythmically as a strong note, and it therefore displaces any *secondary* stress which might otherwise have fallen on the penultimate note; thus

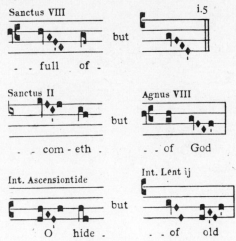

Exceptions may be found; for instance in the psalm-tone endings i. 6 and i. 7 the final note, although it is lengthened, is so clearly a mere extension, that the original rhythm of i. 5 is preserved, e.g.

(iv) The occurrence of a *pressus* (see p. 17) is capable of disturbing the normal secondary stress of a preceding neum only if within its own neum the *pressus* has the effect of making the first note weak. Compare, for instance, the following pair of compound neums:—

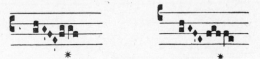

In the first instance the normal accentuation of the opening neum has been thus disturbed.

On the whole, the student need not be greatly exercised as to the position of secondary stresses, especially in his earlier days, as most frequently the act of singing provides its own solution. In practice, it is surprising how seldom the broad rule of a stress at the third note of a 4-note or 5-note neum does not apply.

If more detailed information is sought, the chapters on Rhythm (in relation to the Latin text) in *A Grammar of Plainsong*, published by the Benedictines at Stanbrook Abbey, Worcester, will be found useful.

As to the non-existence of a four-note unit, the consideration of such words in the English text as 'míserable', 'céremonies', 'ínnocency', may lead to a questioning of the finally axiomatic nature of the binary and ternary law. It is maintained in some quarters that simple neums of four and five notes may occasionally be instances of quaternary and quinary feet respectively. Reference may be made to *Latin Hymnody* by Dom Anselm Hughes, O.S.B. (Faith Press). See also *Grammar of Plainsong*, p. 51.

Compound neums consist of the combination of two or more simple neums, and the rhythm of the whole group is recognizable from its composition, the stresses being merely those of the component simple neums as they fall in succession:

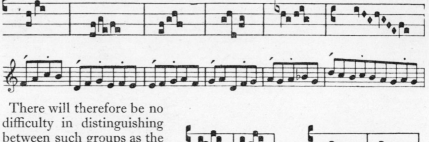

There will therefore be no difficulty in distinguishing between such groups as the following which, though consisting of the same notes, differ in rhythm:

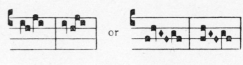

It is useful to remember that the setting of a *virga* at the apex or culminating point of a neum generally signifies a secondary stress at that note. e.g.:

In addition to the natural articulation of compound neums into their elements, a kind of phrasing is sometimes indicated within a compound neum by slight spaces of subdivision, e.g.:—

Lord, have mer - - - - - - - - - - cy.
Ky - ri - e   e - - - ley-son.

The notes immediately preceding the spaces are then subject, as the lay-out of the notes would suggest, to a slight prolongation [1]—a doubling of time-value—and the neums might be transcribed thus:—

In certain recent editions a slight space is also encountered within a simple neum known as the *salicus*:

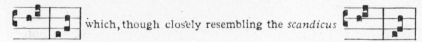

which, though closely resembling the *scandicus*

is distinct, in that a stress is given to the second note. Once again, the spacing makes the accentuation clear, but as in most editions of the English text this distinction is not made, it may be well to bear in mind that when the *scandicus* appears in the form ▉ instead of ▉, the rhythm of the *salicus* may not be incorrect.

There are three circumstances which may disturb the usual accentuation at the beginning of a neum:

1. The occurrence of the *pressus*, i.e., the contact, within a neum, of

---

[1] This prolongation of a note (the *mora vocis*) is indicated in some editions by a full-point after the note concerned, corresponding in idea with the dotting of a note in modern music, thus:—

Ky - ri - e   e - - le - i - son

This device is also used for indicating not only a rallentando before a division bar—

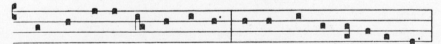

...Great Judge, to op - en thine as-size, To give each hid-den sin its smart,

but the precise point at which the rallentando begins, thus:—

The roy - al ban-ners for-ward go ; The Cross shines forth in mystic glow

C

two notes of the same pitch followed immediately (still within the same neum) by another note, generally a lower one:

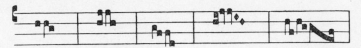

The effect of this meeting is to produce one long note instead of a repeated note, with a strong stress at the expense of the preceding note (if any), thus:—

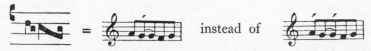

2. In the *salicus* mentioned above, the stress at the second note is transferred from the first note:

3. The *quilisma*, which is weak itself and strengthens the preceding note:

If, as in this example, the *quilisma* is preceded by two notes (a *podatus* or *clivis*) it is usual to dwell on the first note so as to double its length:

Explanation has already been given that a division bar implies a rallentando which will vary in intensity with the importance of the bar. As a general rule it will be confined to the two notes before the bar, or to the last note alone if the penultimate note, either for verbal or musical reasons, is not the stronger of the two. (See footnote p. 17.) The final division bar naturally calls for a more marked rallentando, except when it is employed, as it frequently is, to indicate alternations between groups of singers (chanters and chorus, men and boys), in which case it will be treated as an ordinary full division bar.

Three occasions of stumbling may here be noted for the beginner:
1. It must be remembered that it is always the first note of a two-note neum which receives the accent, while the second note is lighter. There

is a temptation in a rising neum to accent the higher note instead, e.g.:

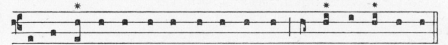

Glo - ry be to the Fa-ther, and to the Son, and to the ho - ly Ghost

It is not in the earliest stages only that care has to be exercised not to stress the second note of the neums marked *.

2. Weak syllables at the ends of phrases must be jealously watched; they easily become leaden. They can hardly be ' taken off ' too lightly.

. . _ I have been in trou - ble :   - - mer - ci - ful and ten - der,

3. Passages of single notes alternating with two-note neums seem to be particularly prone to a mechanical ' crotchet-quaver ' interpretation due to the improper lengthening of the single notes coupled with a hurrying of the neums. For instance, in the Christmas sequence:

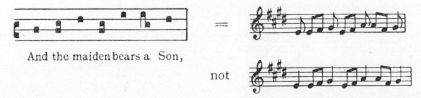

And the maiden bears a Son,

not

Series of two-note neums also offer opportunities for a similar mal-treatment of the rhythm, e.g.:

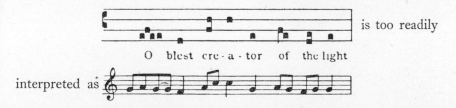

is too readily

O blest cre - a - tor of the light

interpreted as

With regard to pace, except in large resonant buildings, anything appreciably slower for single notes than the deliberate enunciation of distinct natural reading will probably be too slow. The chant should move quickly with a smooth flow and pulse, and with no suggestion of labour. The following exercise may be useful for serving the double purpose of testing the average speed and, so to speak, shaking the rhythm free. Take the words ' Lord have mercy upon us, and incline our hearts to keep this law ' in conjunction with the melody that is now commonly associated with Merbecke's Communion office.

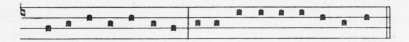

    1. Read the whole sentence aloud in the natural voice, quite simply and distinctly, blurring no syllable, yet clearly retaining the natural speech accentuation.

    2. Repeat the process exactly but in monotone.

    3. Repeat again, still retaining the original pace and rhythm, but applying the melody.

    4. To test, repeat process No. 1.

Choirmasters will find this type of exercise useful for instructional purposes. For strictly syllabic music they may adapt it by making sections of the choir combine processes 1 and 3 simultaneously. Both sections will require careful attention.

The student should now be in possession of sufficiently full elementary knowledge to enable him to give an intelligent interpretation of any plainsong melody. Naturally he will develop his proficiency by practice, and he will certainly find no dearth of exercises if he will set himself the pleasant task of soaking in the pages of *The Ordinary of the Mass; Additional Settings of Certain Canticles; Introits;* and the *English Hymnal.* (See p. ii.)

CHAPTER III

TONALITY

THE MODES

The terrors of the modal system will be reduced by one-half so soon as the novice grasps two very elementary factors, namely:

1. Throughout the whole range of plainsong he has to deal with white notes only; that is to say, the melodies as he will find them written, are all capable of being played on the white notes. In other words, he is dealing with the diatonic scale. The exceptional B flat will be considered later.

2. The division into modes is primarily a method of sorting melodies into classes according to the notes on which they end, *i.e.*, ' finals '.

The need for any such classification becomes at once apparent when it is seen how profoundly the character of a melody is affected by the circumstance of its final note. A rough parallel may serve to illustrate the point. The character or ' flavour ' of the familiar ending of a hymn tune

would have been very different if the ' final ' had been C instead of E flat:

or different again had it been F:

Plainsong melodies fall into four primary classes according to whether they end on D, E, F, or G, corresponding with the old mode-names of Dorian, Phrygian, Lydian, and Mixolydian respectively.

The need, however, for an inner classification or sub-division becomes evident when it is remembered that one octave provides a sufficient range for almost any plainsong melody, and that this octave may be in one of two positions in relation to the final D, E, F, or G, viz., it may rise from the final itself, or from the interval of a fourth below, i.e., A, B, C, or D, according to its class. Each final, then, serves two octaves or modes, the upper of which is known as the ' authentic ' mode, and the lower as the relative ' plagal '. This sub-division is therefore a differentiation of locality.

The eight ecclesiastical modes may be set out thus:

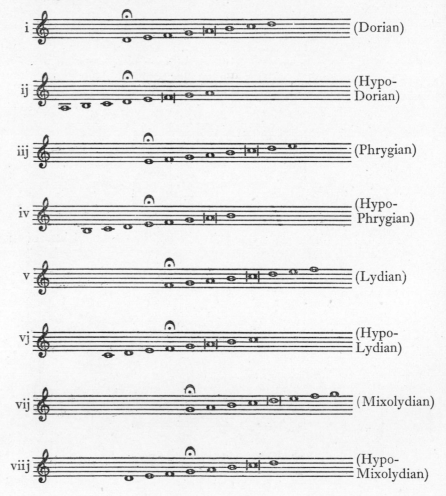

i (Dorian)

ij (Hypo-Dorian)

iij (Phrygian)

iv (Hypo-Phrygian)

v (Lydian)

vj (Hypo-Lydian)

vij (Mixolydian)

viij (Hypo-Mixolydian)

The total result of the twofold classification is a grouping of melodies which, according to their class, impress the ear (some melodies more clearly than others) with certain characteristics best conveyed perhaps by the word ' flavour '.

The modes are still sometimes referred to under the old Greek names, in which case the plagal or lower mode is distinguished by the prefix ' Hypo '. This nomenclature has the advantage of marking the relationship between the pairs of modes (e.g., Dorian and Hypo-Dorian, which must necessarily have much in common in that they have a common final) and is largely retained in connexion with folksong, though here the frequency with which the range exceeds the octave, and the absence of a peculiar 'dominant', make a distinction between authentic and plagal superfluous. A folk tune, therefore, which is classified as ' Dorian ' may quite well be expected to range several notes below its final D. In dealing with the ecclesiastical chant, however, it will be found that the distinction is more marked, and convenience has dictated the simple numerical classification which is now generally accepted, and which will be adhered to throughout these pages.

It will by this time be understood that any first mode melody will consist of notes contained in the first stave of the above table (or a slight extension of it), and will end on its final D; and so on with the other modes.

Two other points must be noticed:

1. Each mode has a ' dominant ', not in the modern sense, but a dominating note which asserts itself constantly in certain melodies of that mode or acts as a central note around which the melody more or less pivots, though the influence of this note is much stronger in certain classes of melody than in others. The dominant is of supreme importance in the psalm tones where it is employed as the reciting note. In the above table it is marked thus: |◁| , and it will be noticed that whereas an authentic mode and its relative plagal have a common final (marked ⌒), the dominants are not the same.

2. The B in every mode is liable to be flattened. This accidental may be regarded as a relaxation (or perhaps a complication) of the strict modal system, and no doubt it owes its origin to a desire to escape from the tritone (B to F), an interval which, even before the harmonic system developed, was increasingly felt to be intolerable. The student will do well to bear in mind that the B flat is, after all, an accidental, and that the less it figures, so much the more clearly is the pure form of the mode preserved.

For purposes of comparison it may now be found useful to transpose the modes so as to reduce them all to a common pitch:

To avoid misunderstanding, it should perhaps be pointed out that in the above scales the first and last notes have no peculiar significance beyond marking the normal range limits of the mode unless they are specially designated as finals, as in the authentic modes.

Several interesting points emerge:

(*a*) In modes i to iv, the final—which is, in a sense, the ' key note ' to which other notes are referred—proceeds upwards to a minor third, thereby imparting a definitely minor character to each of these modes. In modes v to viij, however, the third above the final is major, and their character is correspondingly major. This will inevitably be felt at the close of a melody, and generally throughout its course.

(*b*) A striking feature of modes iij and iv is the minor second above the final. Melodies descending by a semitone on to their final are immediately recognized as belonging to one or other of these modes—to which of the two, will be determined by the ' lie ' of the melody in relation to the final. Melodies in these modes, however, do not necessarily all approach their final from above.

(c) Modes v and vj are the only ones distinguished by a leading note—the final being approached from below by a semitone. All other modes approach the final upwards through a flattened seventh.

(d) The notes of mode viij are identical with mode i. But if the positions of the finals and dominants of these respective modes are noticed, and their functions remembered (i.e., to act as an ' anchor ' and ' pivot ' respectively for the other notes), and further if the characteristic mentioned in (a) above is borne in mind, the dissimilarity of these modes will be evident.

(e) The notes of mode vj are identical with those of the modern major scale. Note carefully, however, the final and the dominant; also the interval between the final and the third note above it.

(f) Mode vij, including its final and dominant, is the modern major scale except for the flattened seventh instead of a leading note—a vital distinction, particularly as melodies lie low in the scale for the most part, and, by means of a downward extension of the mode, approach the final upwards.

FLATTENING THE B.

The effect of flattening the B of any mode will be seen by adding the next available flat to the key signature extended on the right of the above table of transposed modes, and in the case of mode v, by making the sharp a natural. It will at once be observed that there will be a duplication of key signatures, e.g., an added flat in the key signature for mode i produces the ordinary key signature for mode ij. But, as in (d) above, the lowest note of the scale representing mode ij is not the final (as it is in the case of mode i), and further, the dominants differ. Similar comparisons may be made with the other modes.

The result, then, of flattening the B will have a less confusing effect on the modes than on the student. For his comfort let him recollect, however, that the B flat is really an exception, that it will take care of itself when it occurs in a melody, that it may come as a help to him in his accompaniment, but that his first concern is to become familiar with the unadulterated tonality of the mode: that is the atmosphere in which he is to think.

Two points of interest may be noted:

(i) The flattening of the B of mode v (F sharp in the above scale) produces the modern major scale, with its proper key note and dominant. (See (e) above.)

(ii) In mode vij, the flattened B (E flat in the above scale) reproduces the mode i scale, together with its final and dominant. Actually, however, on account of the ' lie ' of the melodies, there is seldom need to flatten the B in mode vij, whereas in mode i the frequent proximity of the notes B and F (the hated tritone interval) accounts for the very common use of the accidental. In fact, the relationship of the two modes is close only in theory. Practically, there can be no confusion. In mode vij the recurrence of the unflattened B (which is a major third above the final) imparts an unmistakably ' major ' character to most melodies (e.g., the Introit for Ascension Day, p. 108), which no occasional accidental can obliterate.

KEY SIGNATURE.

For transcribing a plainsong melody into modern notation the following rule will secure the correct key signature.

Determine a convenient pitch for singing the melody, and employ the ordinary key signature of whatever note is found to fall on the C line. (For exceptions, see appendix to Chapter III). For instance:

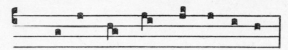

If considerations of pitch demand that the second note should be B flat the key signature required will be that of B flat major.

Or if the melody requires no transposition, the key signature will naturally be that of C major.

Finally a word of encouragement for the young student. The chapter opened hopefully enough, but during its course complications have arisen, and perhaps despondency in the reader. It is good, though, that he should know from the outset the sort of distinctions and characteristics he will have to look for in dealing with the different modes. Let him remember, however, that it is not necessary to grasp all the subtleties of the modal system before making a very good beginning in the accompaniment of plainsong. As a first step it was undoubtedly necessary for him to make the notation and the rhythm his own. These were the doorway through which he must pass; but the modes are given him from above, as a land to explore. At first he will go as he is bidden. Later, his practical experience will help him to move about in them with increasing familiarity, and so he will come to learn their full beauties, to feel at home in them, and to love them—yes, and sometimes, perhaps, to dare step outside them. The years so spent will be happy.

APPENDIX TO CHAPTER III
TRANSPOSED MELODIES

A certain type of melody will be met, the final of which does not correspond with that of the mode under which it is classified. Instances of this are exceptional though not rare, but as the student can become a very useful accompanist without knowing anything whatever of this peculiarity, it has been thought wise to avoid confusing his mind in early days and to confine instruction on this point to an appendix.

An apparently impossible final is evidence that the melody has been transposed up a fourth or a fifth in the plainsong notation with an *approximately* corresponding change of clef. Approximately so, for the reason that an exact transposition of *all* the notes of the mode cannot be effected by a mere change in the position of the clef.

The object of this transposition was to make use of a note which normally did not figure in the mode.

Mode iij

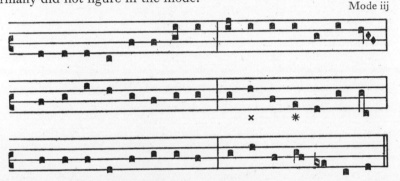

This is an example of a third mode melody with an F sharp added to it by a process of transposition.

If the position of the C is ignored for the moment, and, bearing in mind that the final of the mode is E (as is therefore the first note also, in this instance), the tune is read through accordingly (i.e., without transposition), it will be found that in the fourth division the fourth note is an F occurring in unpleasantly close proximity to an earlier B—the intolerable tritone interval. Clearly something must be done. The remedy is to sharpen the F, and the means of effecting this is to shift the clef so as to transpose the melody a fourth up. What was an F now becomes a B flat. Omit the flat sign and the effect of an F sharp is achieved. This manipulation allows for the characteristic F of the mode (the semitone above the final) being preserved when required, by the use of the flat (♭) which is seen thus used in the last line.

This transposing up a fourth in order to get the effect of an F sharp, and a similar transposing up a fifth to get the effect of a permanent B flat, or of an E flat by flattening the transposed B, is not uncommon. A further example of the former may be seen in the Introit for Trinity xij, and of the latter in the Introit for the Sunday after Ascension, or in Hymns 2, 214, or 261 (E.H.):—

This last instance is interesting because, as the B of the untransposed mode (F as transposed) never occurs, the transposition is entirely unnecessary, and merely bears witness to a second mode habit. The evidence of transposition is always clear, of course, in the misleading position of the final; A, for instance, is the final of no mode. The final of mode ij is D.

The question here is: how is this manipulation of the modes going to affect the accompanist?

Surely little violence will be done if the accompanist, taking the chant at its face value, uses the ordinary key signature that he would under the normal rule (p. 26). He will at least be using notes which are employed in the melody. It should be borne in mind, however, that the transposition has usually been made, not in order to alter the tonality of the whole, but to provide for a fleeting exceptional note. Therefore, if the pure tonality is to be strictly preserved, the accompanist will have, by a mathematical process, to modify his key signature as follows:

Melody transposed 4th up: allow one sharp less (or one flat more).

Melody transposed 5th up: allow one sharp more (or one flat less).

Example:

If considerations of pitch dictate that the note on the C line shall be D, the normal rule provides for the D major key signature of two sharps, thus:

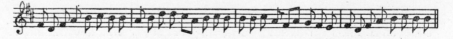

But as the final appears to be A, whereas a second mode melody actually ends on D, there must have been a transposition of a fifth up. Therefore the key signature must bear an additional sharp, with a G natural as an accidental in the third division:

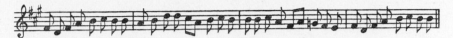

The former key signature will suffice, but it is good for the accompanist to remember that the G sharp is the normal, and that he may use it accordingly in the course of his accompaniment.

Lest it still be felt that requirement for this modification is pedantic, the following instance may convince:

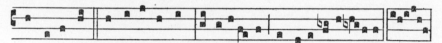

Seek ye the Lord, while he may be found: call ye up-on him while he is near, al-le-lu-ya.   iv. 4

This fourth mode Advent antiphon is transposed up a fourth in order to gain the effect of F sharp in the third section (represented, of course, by B). The normal tonality, however, is restored to the next section by the use of the flat giving the very characteristic fall of a semitone on to the final. Now this F of the mode is a most characteristic note, so much so that the use of the F sharp in an accompaniment should be shunned at all costs unless a specific licence is granted, as it is in this antiphon. Suppose, then, that the F sharp of the mode is allowed to figure in the key signature of the accompaniment. The antiphon leads directly into its psalm without any break. Is the F sharp to be used there also, as a matter of course? Shall we, for instance, accompany the fourth ending thus:

Surely not, unless its tonality is to be entirely sacrificed. The accompanist must be on the lookout for these transpositions, settle his key signature in accordance with the true mode, and depart from it only if it is necessary in the immediate neighbourhood of the F sharp effect. A little more latitude is naturally allowable where the transposition is made in order to flatten B's; however, the B natural should not be suppressed.

The rule, then, is clear, and its strict application in mode iv is called for. Whether in other cases the F sharp or the E flat may be drawn on more freely is a slightly different consideration. Being in the nature of a licence, its use must be governed by choice rather than by accident; the rule at least should be known.

Incidentally these remarks remove a misconception as to the use of the C clef, namely, that melodies were transposed in order to bring them within a reasonable singing pitch. On the contrary, the 𝄡 has no significance of absolute pitch, and it has been shown that transposition arose from entirely different causes. It is interesting, too, to observe that as the sharp sign was not brought into existence until the fifteenth century, transposition was the only method available for securing that occasional accidental.

Complications may be resented by the student, but, lest he grudge unduly, it may soften him to recollect that when the melody was evolved, the writers can hardly have said: ' Now let us write something in a transposed mode so as to make it more difficult '. Rather the melodies took shape in the minds and voices of people who, maybe, were not concerned with writing them down; at any rate not in a four-line stave. The tritone effects would get smoothed away by an instinctive process. When the time came to catch those creations in black and white, the only means of preserving an F sharp or an E flat was to transpose the mode by a manipulation of the clef.

CHAPTER IV

THE ACCOMPANIMENT

1. Negative.
2. The kind of chord to use.
3. Vertical Aspect: Harmony in relation to the rhythm—
   (a) Where to place chords.
   (b) Passage from chord to chord.
   (c) Examples in detail.
4. Horizontal Aspect: Harmony in relation to the melodic line—
   (a) Number of parts.
   (b) Harmonic basis as an accompaniment.
   (c) Other decorative forms of accompaniment.
5. Registration.

1. NEGATIVE.

It cannot be too clearly emphasized that the melody is complete without any accompaniment whatever. Attention has already been drawn to this in Chapter I, and here it may further be urged that in no service, whether festival or otherwise, should all the plainchant be tied to an accompaniment as a matter of course. The choir responses at Matins and Evensong, the Litany, the Gloria before the gospel, the Sursum Corda, and all sung Amens afford opportunities which should gladly be seized for allowing the organ to be silent. Quite apart from the intrinsic beauty and the gain of variety, the ability which the singers will achieve to respond naturally, as a matter of habit, is a most valuable asset. It would, indeed, be well to regard the sum of these as an irreducible minimum of unaccompanied plainsong, which would form a foundation for singing at least the office hymn and the psalms during Lent and Passiontide without the organ. The choirmaster who will have the courage to experiment in this direction will perhaps be surprised to find that as the next Lent comes round, he will positively welcome its musical austerities.

2. THE KIND OF CHORD TO USE.

Two elements require consideration in choosing the chords which are to be used for the accompaniment of plainsong:
   (i) Material available;
   (ii) Manner of construction.

   (i) *Material.*—Plainsong melodies are cast in the eight ecclesiastical modes, which admit the use of no accidentals other than the flattening of the B.[1] That is to say, a definite limitation has been imposed and accepted

---

[1] And the comparatively rare exception of an F sharp or E flat arrived at by a process of transposition. This is dealt with in the appendix to Chapter III.

in selecting the material: certain notes have been rejected. It follows that the same kind of discrimination which underlay the choice of material for the melody must also be exercised in forming the chords used to accompany it, unless melody and accompaniment are to diverge in colour and be out of sympathy. The chords, then, will consist exclusively of notes contained in the mode of the melody.

The term ' modal accompaniment ' has no doubt done good service as a scarecrow to frighten away the timid, yet the thing itself need cause no terror. The first step by which it will be attained is to determine the key signature of the accompaniment in accordance with the rule in Chapter III (p. 26) and to keep rigidly within its confines except for the permissible use of an additional flat or one sharp less, which will, of course, represent the flattening of the B. It is true that there are other considerations, but they are not first in order of importance for the beginner, and they may be deferred to the later stage to which they more properly belong.

(ii) *Construction.*—Frugal diet suggests simple cookery. Further, it should require no demonstration that if the accompaniment is to be a suitable vehicle for an ancient melody, it should lean away from modern harmonies. It should at least have a closer affinity with the harmonic developments of the early polyphonic school than with later forms.

The severest rules are the best, and may be summed up as follows:

Two chords only should be used, viz.:—

(1) The common chord;

(2) Its first inversion. The second inversion is admissible only in the form of a suspension, properly prepared, but it is invariably better to substitute a 4 to 3 or a 6 to 5, thus—

(3) The first inversion of the imperfect triad may be admitted, but as a less staple form of diet. Free use may be made of

(4) Suspensions, properly prepared—4 to 3 (as above), 7 to 6, 9 to 8.

(5) The discord arising from the use of the appoggiatura (see A in Ex. p. 35) is not to be forbidden, though it should be exceptional. In early stages it is best avoided altogether. Its use will be referred to later (p. 77).

(6) Plain octaves.

Such is the accompanist's stock-in-trade. The catalogue is incomplete, however, without a statement that a large proportion of the notes of the melody will be treated as passing notes (a), auxiliary notes (b), and notes of anticipation (c).

The way is now clear for determining *where* the chords are to be placed —a consideration which is at the very root of any satisfactory accompaniment. The chord ill selected is less harmful than the chord ill placed.

3. VERTICAL ASPECT.—Harmony in relation to the rhythm—

(*a*) *Where to place chords.* If the above examples are analysed, it will be noticed firstly, that conforming with the foregoing rule, all the chords employed are common chords (5), first inversions (6), or prepared suspensions (S); secondly, that the use of chords is economical. In the first example 11 chords have been used to accompany 25 melody notes, and in the second only 10. The notes which have no fresh chord of their own are treated simply as passing notes, auxiliary notes, notes of anticipation, or harmony notes over a standing bass.

Now an essential characteristic of any plainsong melody is its fluency, and its right to flow easily must be defended at all costs. Any form of accompaniment, therefore, which impedes movement must be rigorously

D

excluded. In ordinary circumstances it should take not more than ten seconds to sing the above melody; and any more liberal use of chords will unquestionably have the effect of weighing it down, and retarding its free movement, largely on account of the sheer difficulty of playing a quicker succession of chords. For example, an additional chord at the third note of the above Kyrie clearly has a deadening effect:

and still more fatal would be the misapplied energy of such an opening as—

On the contrary, it may be seen that a more rigid economy would enable the melody to shake itself even freer, e.g.:—

This has reduced the proportion to 7 to 25, and in so far as it liberates the light flow of the rhythm it is satisfactory. On the whole, chords to melody notes in a proportion of 1 to 3 is a suitable sort of test standard to be borne in mind, though opportunities of using fewer chords will be sought, whilst, on the other hand, circumstances may demand greater liberality—for instance, in the psalm-tone endings.

If a word of apology is needed for the old chord-per-note accompaniments of half a century or more ago, which so successfully obliterated the character of the melodies, it should be remembered that they arose quite inevitably in early revival days, when patience in research had not borne its full fruit, and when there was no adequate guidance as to the traditional manner of singing the chant—a free verbal rhythm pressing through a quickly flowing melody. Even yct, some of the hymn books at present in popular use seem to have found it unaccountably difficult to detach themselves from this uninformed manner,

How shall a given allowance of chords be distributed? It is evident that if only a comparatively small proportion of the melody notes are going to receive fresh chords, the accompaniment itself must make some contribution to the rhythm of the whole, for each chord as it occurs will have the effect of creating a fresh pulse or accent of its own.

For instance, to revert to a melody used as an example in Chapter II:

The melody, as it stands without words, has no rhythm, but the first accompaniment, by the distribution of its chords, naturally suggests an accent at the third and sixth notes. That is to say, the first accompaniment is less congruous with the words ' and ascènded into hèaven ' than with the words ' and the thìrd day he ròse again '.

Now it is perfectly true that it is to the voices that the prime responsibility is entrusted for establishing the verbal and musical rhythm of the melody. If, however, the accompaniment introduces accents which are foreign, to that extent will the rhythm of the melody tend to become clouded.

It follows, therefore, that fresh chords or changes of bass should as far as possible coincide with accents in the rhythm of the melody. A couple more examples will drive the point home:

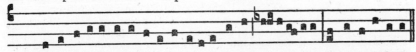

Who with the Father and the Son to-geth-er is wor-ship-ped and glo-ri-fi-ed: who spake by the Prophets.

D 2

- - we ac-know-ledge thee to be the Lord. All the earth doth wor-ship thee, the Fa-ther ev-er-last-ing.

It should here be pointed out that the converse does not necessarily hold true: that is to say, an accent in the melody, whether verbal or musical, does not in itself demand a change of chord. For instance, in the second example the comparatively strong accents at * might have been marked by a change of chord, but it was chosen not to do so, not only because there was no need, and economy of chords is valuable, but also because the filling in of these blanks would have established too great a regularity of tread throughout the whole accompaniment to allow a feeling of repose. This example is also useful, incidentally, for showing at the third chord how it is sometimes difficult to avoid changing the bass at a comparatively unaccented note. Both verbally and musically, however, a change at ‘ be ’ is more satisfactory than at either of its weaker neighbours ‘ to ’ or ‘ the ’. Perhaps the whole passage would have been better accompanied in some such manner as this:

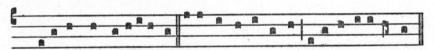

- - we ac-know-ledge thee to be the Lord. All the earth doth wor-ship thee, the Fa-ther ev-er-last-ing.

The idea of emphasizing accented syllables by a change of chord is, of course, by no means peculiar to the accompaniment of plainsong. Exactly the same principle underlies the bulk of recitative accompaniment in oratorio, and a parallel treatment is not uncommon in the modern song. It is interesting to note how completely the idea is applied in the following quotation from Martin Shaw’s ‘ Columbine’s Grave ’ (Cramer).

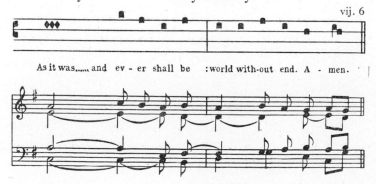

All accented notes, then, furnish opportunities (which may or may not be used) for a change of chord. In addition, the division bar implies a rallentando—slight or marked, according to the degree of the division—reaching back to the nearest stressed note, and indicates correspondingly a locality within which chords may be used more freely. The rallentando may be confined to a single final note or it may begin a little earlier, but in any case the note immediately preceding a division bar, irrespective of all other considerations, is naturally subject to a slight lengthening and accordingly provides an opportunity (which, again, may or may not be used) for a change of chord. Before a final double bar this opportunity will certainly be used; here indeed, where the rallentando is very marked and is pushed back usually for three or four notes, chords may well be used fairly liberally.

vij. 6

When your fa - thers tempted me : pro-ved me   and saw my   works.

Coupling the foregoing considerations with the analysis of rhythm in Chapter II a position is reached which may be outlined as follows:

(i) There are no laws demanding a change of chord at any note, but

(ii) Always keeping in mind the need for economy in the use of chords, there are certain points where one is *entitled* to make a change, and from these points a selection must be made. The ' entitling points ' or ' possible points ' are:—

(1) Strong syllables (single notes).

(2) A stressed note in a neum.

(3) The close of a phrase (the rallentando).

ANALYSIS OF NEUMS.

All. The first note is always stressed.

>The second note is always weak (but this may coincide with (3) above).

3 *note.* The middle note is weakest.

>Never use more than two chords; more usually one only.

4 *note.* The third note is liable to a slight stress; but a division bar immediately following may draw this stress to the last note (see p. 15). The use of three chords is usually excessive unless (3) above applies.

5 *note.* The secondary stress will fall on the third or fourth note according to the neum's character and context (see p. 14). Two chords should be sufficient; one may do better.

Compound neums generally analyse themselves.

N.B.—The normal accentuation of a neum may be disturbed by the presence of a *pressus* or a *quilisma*. See also *salicus* (p. 17) and ' Compound Neums ' (p. 16).

(b) *Passage from chord to chord*. Approaching a fresh chord.
The nature of the chords at the accompanist's disposal provides that
every fresh chord will be a concord unless it is a prepared suspension[1]
(p. 32)—an instance of passing from concord to discord:

A new chord must never be approached by a discord unless the note
forming the discord falls within one of the following three categories.
In each case it will be observed to be a weak note:
   (i) A note of anticipation:

   (ii) A passing note, in the particular sense of an unessential note moving
stepwise to a harmony note in the same direction in which it was
approached:

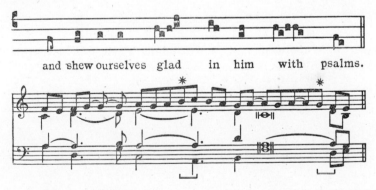

---

[1] The appoggiatura is dealt with at p. 77.

(iii) An auxiliary note, i.e., a passing note returning to the harmony note whence it started:

... and the na-tions un - der our feet

It will therefore be inadmissible to approach a fresh chord thus:

God of God

That is to say, it is not sufficient for the fresh chord to be approached stepwise in the melody in order to entitle the note of approach to form a discord, whereas had the B fallen within either category ii or iii above, the same discord would have been permissible, i.e.,

or

Similarly, in the sequence for All Saints, it will not be permissible to approach the fresh chord at ' min-' thus:

. - Of the Spi - rit's min - is - try, . -

A better treatment would be:

The approach to ' Spi- ', however, in the previous harmony cannot be so readily dismissed as not fulfilling the orthodox requirements, for the B at ' the ', although it is not strictly a note of anticipation, is yet anticipatory of the B within the following chord, and may therefore be regarded as classifiable under that category. Such an approach is clearly preferable to:

It is not the nature of the discord which rules this example out, but the fact that it anticipates nothing, for had the same discord led on thus :

it would have been perfectly satisfactory.

Such anticipatories, then, may be allowed, but it is useful to note that the effect would have been improved had the C natural (with which the B forms a discord) not been doubled:

(In this connexion, see notes on three-part work, p. 49.)

By this time it may have been noticed that the restrictions laid down as to the manner of passing from chord to chord might have been covered by a more general rule at an earlier stage to the effect that all notes of the melody which do not receive a fresh chord must form either harmony notes (concords), or discords in the shape of notes of anticipation, passing notes, or auxiliary notes. The rule does, in fact, hold good, but attention has deliberately been focussed upon the manner of approaching a fresh chord because it is at this point, in the actual process of harmonizing a melody, that the need is chiefly felt for analysing notes. In other words, a weak discord may more safely be trusted to take care of itself when occurring *inside* the duration of a chord than when it is in the act of approaching a fresh chord.

(c) Examples in detail.

It may now be found instructive to take a fairly simple melody as an example, and in successive detailed stages to construct an accompaniment so as to illustrate the application of the foregoing rules.

EXAMPLE 1, from *Te Deum* (solemn):

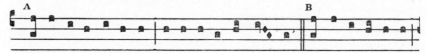

The gló-ri-ous cóm-pa-ny of the A-pós-tles práise thee The good-ly fél-low-ship

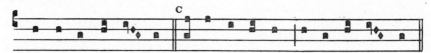

of the Pró-phets práise thee The nó-ble ár-my of Már-tyrs práise thee.

The example divides itself into three similar sentences, marked A, B, and C.

i. The natural verbal accentuation, which is our first concern, is shown as marked above.

ii. In addition, the first note of each neum is stressed, i.e., at 'The', '—tles', 'praise', 'The', 'fel—', '—phets', 'praise', 'The', 'ar-', '—tyrs', and 'praise'.

iii. At the three cadences marked by the double division bars (here used to indicate the alternation of contrasting voices) the final note is dwelt on slightly. To a less degree, the same applies to the intermediate bars. The opening of each fresh division is also quite naturally a possible opportunity for a fresh chord.

Combining these stresses and rallentandos it is found that the 'entitling points' or 'possible points' for changes of chord are as marked below:

A suitable change of chord at any of these points will not in itself be improper, but to change at all will produce far too restless an effect. Economy must therefore be exercised. The weaker stresses will quite naturally be the first points to be discarded and the strongest verbal accents will become our lodestars, as it were. These will subdivide the melody into joints or sections, and the first general principle will be to apply one chord to each section, with the option of additional chords at division bars or to mark the rallentando at a cadence. This will be found to be a good working method, though obviously it does not demand rigid application, as of a law. Long neums, for instance, most frequently demand some change of chord within them; the more elaborate the melody, the greater will be the call to modify the principle. Conversely it will be remembered that even for a strong verbal accent a fresh chord is not inevitable.

In the first sentence (A) the sections may be marked thus:

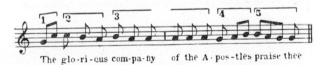

If these sections then are, roughly, to be accompanied by one chord each, and if, save for the already stated exceptions (p. 39), changes of chord are always to be made by moving from concord to concord, chords must be chosen which are closely related to the notes of the section. The first and last notes of each section will naturally be first looked to for suggesting a suitable chord.

The sections of the example may now be dealt with in detail.

Sentence A

Section 1. As these two notes are elements of the common chord of C, they suggest the use of that chord or its first inversion—in whatever position may be convenient.

Section 2. Clearly suggests the chord of A minor or its first inversion. The chord of F major will be less satisfactory as the passing note B will form the unpleasant tritone interval with the bass F.

Sections 4 and 5 each suggest the chord of E minor or G major or their first inversions.

Section 3. The repetition of the A, interrupted by a division bar, suggests the use of more than one chord. The first A may be regarded as a weak note of anticipation and may be treated accordingly. Whether we place a new chord both before and after the division bar will be a matter of choice. Economy would suggest that one change is enough ; or we might manage a change of chord without a change of bass ; or yet again, ' of the A- ' might be accompanied by the bare octave.

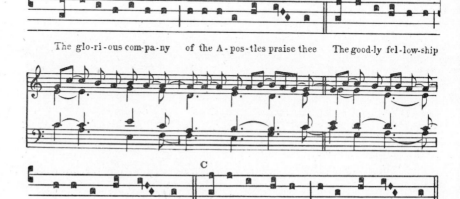

The glo-ri-ous com-pa-ny   of the A-pos-tles praise thee   The good-ly fel-low-ship

of the Pro-phets praise thee.   The no-ble ar-my   of Mar-tyrs praise thee.

Sentence A has been closed by a fresh chord. The continuation of the previous chord of G major would have been satisfactory, and may be seen thus used before the opening of sentence C.

Sentence B.

The opening section is common to sentences A, B, and C. The second section (' goodly ') is an opportunity for a 4 to 3 suspension which has been properly prepared. ' Fellowship ' is amply served by one chord, and the possible chords to consider for this purpose would be common chords or first inversions which contain A and comply with the key signature, i.e., the chord A minor, D minor, F major, or their first inversions, though the chord of F major would be less satisfactory for the reason indicated under section 2 above (p. 43). That of A minor fits into the previous harmony with a minimum of movement and the suspension of the inner part (D) at ' fellow ' provides a suitable decoration. ' Of the ' may, but need not, have a fresh chord. ' Prophets ' corresponds with '—postles ' in the previous division. Here, however, the opportunity has been seized of passing from discord to concord through the weak note of anticipation B.

Sentence C.

Instead of accompanying ' noble ' by a 6 to 5 on E (which is what the notes themselves suggest) the weak passing note B has been allowed to form a discord. The accompaniment of ' praise ' by another part moving in contrary motion is characteristic and useful. On the other hand, the importance and nature of the word, combined with its close proximity to the double bar, might well justify some broader treatment, such as:

EXAMPLE 2. A rather more elaborate melody—the introit antiphon for the Commemoration of All Souls:—

The treatment of this melody will be very similar to the previous example, except that as it consists very largely of fairly long compound neums, it will fall less naturally into the ' chord sections ' which the more nearly syllabic melody suggested. However, if each compound neum is regarded as one such complete section, capable of subdivision if necessary, the application of our general principles will not be found difficult.

As before, the verbal accentuation will claim first attention, and the strong syllables '—ter—', ' grant ', ' Lord ', ' light ', '—pet—', ' shine ', will almost inevitably call for new chords. Next, the division bars marking new musical phrases will be obvious opportunities for new chords, as also the rallentandos leading to them.

In addition there are five compound neums, some falling on weak syllables and some on strong. The general scheme of chord sections now arrived at is as follows:—

Before constructing an accompaniment, a glance may be taken at the five compound neums, which will probably not all be satisfied with a single chord each.

The first one, '—ter—', consists of two simple neums, but the occurrence of the *pressus* at their junction (see p. 18) disturbs what would otherwise be the normal accentuation, and causes a strong stress to fall upon the second note of the whole group (G).

' Them ': The *quilisma* (see p. 18) at the fifth note clearly defines the accentuation of this compound neum: the secondary stresses will be at G and B flat (the quilisma's neighbours) and changes of chord, if necessary, will be at either or both of these points.

' Shine ' is a slightly elaborated form of ' them ' and consists of the neum just discussed with the addition of a slight prefix. Its formation as printed (with a space between the second and third notes) shows the first note of the original neum retaining its stress.

' O ' and ' on ', which are identical, are a form which is very commonly encountered and presents no difficulty. As its formation suggests, the third note (the culminating *virga*) receives a secondary stress. The essence of the neum is the ascending scale descending again to the note from which it started. Its final note is merely an anticipation.

The application of chords is now a matter of no difficulty. Everything
before the first double bar being 'chanted', the word 'Rest' will
require no accompaniment.

Sections 1, 2, and 3 may be harmonized in a variety of ways.

Section 1 suggests the chords of F major or D minor, or their first
inversions, or the neum might open with the chord of B flat and the
last note, being a note of anticipation, might form a discord with the
bass. Plain octaves of course are always available, and they frequently
serve very well for an opening.

Section 2. It would be possible to accompany the whole neum with
one chord by opening with a prepared 7 to 6 suspension.

Some less assertive opening for this neum is to be preferred, however,
especially as the rhythmic climax, coming as it does at the second note
(i.e., at the *pressus*), weakens the force of the first note. If only one
chord is to be used then, it should be placed at the second note.
Nevertheless, the strong verbal accent at the first note would clearly
justify a fresh chord there, and those of A minor, D minor, and F major
are all available, or their first inversions; and for the second part of the
neum the most suitable accompaniment is evidently the 6 to 5 figure
over B flat. Another way of dealing with the opening sections would
be to use the chord of D minor or F major to accompany 'e—', and to
retain it for the beginning of the next neum, merely moving an inner
part to coincide with the verbal stress encountered at '—ter—', thus:

Sections 3, 7, and 13. The notes suggest a 6 to 5 over B flat, or a
prepared 4 to 3 suspension; or the slight rallentando before a division
bar will justify the use of two chords.

Section 4. See Section 1. One chord will suffice, but a second may be
required at 'un—' if the chord of B flat is used at 'grant'.

Section 5. Clearly one chord will not suffice, as the accented B flat,
which is in the nature of a climax, will form too violent a discord with

any single chord which the rest of the notes in the neum suggest. The change of chord had better be made at this point then, though a change at the first G instead would be perfectly satisfactory. The first five notes almost cry out to stand over a bass C so that the A and G in the melody will form a 6 to 5 or 5 to 6 as they occur. This device, in fact, is so frequently applicable throughout all plainsong accompaniment that it is hardly possible to overestimate the usefulness of the formula:

and its developments.

Sections 6 and 12. Apart from the G's which are always weak passing notes or anticipations, the notes of the neums are F. A. F, suggesting the chords of D minor, F major, or their first inversions.

Section 9. Each neum may have a separate chord, or one chord will suffice, in which case the remarks immediately above will apply.

Section 10. One chord will suffice here, and it will naturally be a 6 to 5 over B flat with the weak A as an auxiliary note. Or the slight dwelling on the note before the half bar may suggest a second chord at '—al', in which case, as the preceding note is an anticipation, the first chord will be a ' G ' sort of chord: an opportunity of introducing the B natural of the mode by using the chord of G major, despite the tritone effect with the weak F preceding '—al '.

Section 11. The remarks on Section 5 will apply precisely. Two chords will still suffice for the long neum, the ' 6 to 5 formula ' being applicable throughout until the B flat. At this point the chord of G minor suggests itself. The note of anticipation at ' up—' may be allowed to form a discord, though this is better avoided by the simple device shown in the example below—another example of the 6 to 5 formula:

Quite properly, the closing chord is that of the final of the mode. At the end of the neum for the first ' them ' an additional chord has been used which might have been dispensed with had the previous chord been that of G minor. Whilst a single chord would have sufficed, there is no objection to a second chord which makes for a little harmonic variety and, as there is but a slight movement of parts, does not hinder the rhythm of the chant.

The above treatment of these two examples must not create the impression that it is the accompanist's duty to subject every melody to a rigid application of a mathematical formula from which no deviation may be tolerated. The intention is rather to indicate a line of approach and to illustrate the kind of analytical process which must be at the foundation of any satisfactory method of accompaniment. It shows, in fact, the sort of eye the accompanist is to cultivate for his melodies.

4 HORIZONTAL ASPECT.—Harmony in relation to the melodic line.

(a) *Number of Parts.*

If the melody is of an essentially light and flowing character borne on a sort of open framework of harmony, it will not be difficult to see that the supporting chords need not be massive, either in volume or texture. So far, most of the examples of accompaniment have been written in four parts, and this no doubt will be regarded as the normal manner. Five parts may occasionally be employed in special circumstances, but it is better to reduce the number of parts than to add to them. Three-part harmony may and should be used freely. There is no need to be fettered to a complete four-part or three-part scheme. Having embarked on a musical sentence in four parts, it is pleasant to drop into three parts (or even two) and back again, especially if by so doing, it will decrease the movement of parts and help the flow. It will frequently be found that short stretches of three-part harmony will have this effect, and may steer round faulty progressions.

E

E.H. No. 58   Mode ij.

O Boundless Wisdom, God most high,
O Maker of the earth and sky,
Who bid'st the parted waters flow
In heaven above, on earth below:

Further, it will be found that there are many occasions when a fragment
of three-part writing will slip along and admit of chord-changes at
normally unwelcome places, whereas a rigid four-part exercise would
have been depressingly ponderous.

Introit: Maundy Thursday   iv

But   as   for   us   it be - ho - veth us   to   glo - ry

in the Cross of our Lord Je - sus Christ &c.

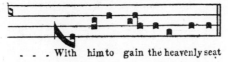

Rosy Sequence (E. H. 238)

. . . . With him to gain the heavenly seat

As an illustration of the economy in movement gained by a little three-part work, it is interesting to watch the hands while playing the last example, and then to repeat the process with the same harmony cast in four parts.

The comparison is convincing on the physical count alone. It is interesting also to see that in its four-part form, the accompaniment has become too cumbered with chords, and calls for remodelling. At least the chord at ' the ' would have to be discarded, whereas in the three-part manner the flow of the melody is entirely unhindered.

(b) Harmonic Basis as an Accompaniment.

It has so far been assumed that the melody will be preserved note for note in the accompaniment. Practical experience, however, will very soon indicate that, on the contrary, occasions frequently arise when the omission of certain notes not only is perfectly natural but positively

E 2

assists the flow of the whole. Instances of the simplest nature are frequently met in the psalm tones, e.g., Tone viij, 2nd ending:

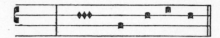

While the normal note for note accompaniment is perfectly satisfactory:

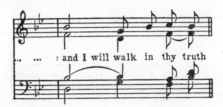

there is a distinct gain if the voices are allowed to move independently, thus:

This not only gives greater freedom to the voices, but, by reducing movement, makes for that restful effect which is characteristic of good plainsong accompaniment.

Independent melody notes may equally well rise above the accompaniment:

Nor need they be confined to single notes, or to concords, though if discords they must be passing notes, auxiliary notes, or notes of anticipation.

but not

where the C as here treated does not fall within any of the required categories.

In all these cases, the omission of notes has been occasioned by the shape of the melody: the accompaniment makes a short cut across a loop.

Such treatments are quite elementary—almost inevitable, indeed, where voices have been trained to move reasonably freely—and may well be encouraged.

The idea, however, can be considerably extended. It is obvious that if the accompaniment of the above example is satisfactory, equally so would it be in the form—

or simply:

or yet again, if a little more movement is felt to be wanted:

In fact, the accompaniment has now presented itself in a new form, which, conceived as a harmonic background against which the melody is allowed to move without the restriction of being tied down note by note, embodies rather more adequately the essential idea of accompaniment than does the stricter harmonization. An accompaniment may well be built up entirely in this manner, woven round about its melody, yet preserving an almost separate entity. It presupposes that the voices are capable of moving with that perfect independence to which it actually contributes. It may be intrinsically beautiful without overstepping the bounds of decorum. Ideally it will not be drawn on as the staple diet, but it may quite well alternate with the stricter and more normal form. Clearly, the accompanist is not committed to one form alone, even within a musical sentence—as a glance at the order of its practical development will remind him. Most happily, perhaps, different forms will be blended and merged in a manner which will be the natural outcome of practical experience.

The essential principles of chord application are identical for both forms. No additional rules are called for, but a few points may be borne in mind:—

i The whole accompaniment may, if desired, move clear of the melody either above or below. Its range is not restricted.

ii If coinciding approximately with the range of the melody, the ' track ' of the melody need not be confined to one part—alto, tenor, etc.

iii If suitable, the accompaniment may move parallel with the track of the melody, an octave above or below.

iv It is not essential for a chord to contain the melody note which it supports.

v An occasional contraction into two parts is frequently useful and pleasant. So is a rest.

vi Few parts, stepwise movement, and the tying over of a part (especially the ' soprano ') are all conditions which, either separately or still more so in combination, facilitate the satisfactory placing of a new chord at a normally unacceptable point.

vii Usually the smaller the interval by which each part moves, the more will smooth running be secured. This, of course, applies to all forms of plainsong accompaniment.

viii The nature of such an accompaniment forbids a heavy use of the organ. Most frequently the registration should be of the lightest variety, especially for supporting boys' voices. The function of the accompaniment is not to compete, but to form a moving background, often of a very delicate nature. (See p. 63.)

Examples may be found more stimulating than instructions, and in those which follow most of the above points are illustrated. In some cases an additional accompaniment of the normal order has been added for the sake of variety and comparison.

Psalm 45. v. 11.   vj.

Hearken, O daughter, and consider; in-cline thine ear: forget also thine own people and thy father's house.

Creed.

And was in-car-nate by the Ho-ly Ghost   of the Vir-gin Ma-ry : and was made man

E.H. 169   i

1 Blessèd City, heavenly Salem,
    Vision dear of peace and love,
Who, of living stones upbuilded,
    Art the joy of heaven above,
And, with Angel cohorts circled,
    As a bride to earth dost move !

2 From celestial realms descending,
    Bridal glory round her shed,
To his presence, decked with jewels,
    By her Lord shall she be led:
All her streets, and all her bulwarks,
    Of pure gold are fashionèd.

E.H. 58 (see also p. 50)   ij

2 The streams on earth, the clouds in heaven,
  By thee their ordered bounds were given,
  Lest 'neath th' untempered fires of day
  The parchèd soil should waste away.

Rosy Sequence (E.H. 238)

6. I seek for Je-sus in re-pose When round my heart its chambers close;

7. With Mary in the morn-ing gloom I seek Je-sus at the tomb

A-broad, and when I shut the door, I long for Je - sus ev-er-more.

For him, with love's most earnest cry I seek with heart and not with eye.

Magnificat
viij. 1. solemn

(c) Other decorative forms of accompaniment

When dealing with the more decorative manners of accompaniment, a distinct form should be noticed in which the whole melody, or a section of it, is retained note for note in a part other than the soprano. During the course of a psalm, canticle, or hymn, an occasional appearance of the melody in the tenor or bass gives a pleasant touch of variety, and the same method may, of course, be applied to short stretches of any other form of plainchant, though its value is rather less in non-repetitive forms. On the whole this manner of treatment will be regarded as exceptional, especially if prominence is given to the melody by the use of registration of a contrasting colour. Two points may be noticed:

i Where the melody appears in the tenor, it will be found that if the harmony is allowed to run into five parts when required, a pleasantly easy flow may often be more readily secured than if the accompaniment is regarded as a four-part exercise. Consecutive fifths and octaves with inner parts need cause no distress in these circumstances.

ii A melody appearing in the bass is best left unfortified by pedals unless it is of a simple nature. The effect is generally too lumbering.

In both of the above cases there is a tendency to multiply movement, which must be watched.

For other than quite simple melodies, spontaneous harmonization at the organ in this form demands considerable skill, and even experienced hands may find it worth while to make written preparation.

As before, most of the examples which follow include instances of more normal workings, for the sake of comparison and added interest.

Psalm 14

5. Their throat is an open sepulchre, with their tongues have they de - ceiv - ed : the poison of asps is under their lips

6. Their mouth is full of curs-ing and bit-ter-ness: their feet are swift to shed blood

7. Destruction & unhappiness is in their ways, and the way of peace have they not known : there is no fear of God be-fore their eyes

C.F.

Benedictus

Tonus Peregrinus

Notes omitted if not required by words

6. To perform the oath which he sware to our forefather Abraham: that he would give us.

7. That we being delivered out of the hand of our enemies: might serve him with-out fear

C.F.

In holiness and righteousness be-fore him: all the days of our life.

9. And thou Child shalt be called the Prophet of the Highest: for thou shalt go be-fore the face of the Lord to pre-pare his ways

C. F.

Gloria I

- - - We - praise   thee,   We   bless   thee,   we   wor - ship   thee,

- - -

we glo-ri-fy thee, we give   thanks to   thee   for   thy great glo-ry, &c.

E. H. No. 176   viij

2 Ye servants who once bore the light
 Of Gospel truth o'er heathen night,
 Still may your work that light impart,
 To glad our eyes and cheer our heart.

3 O God, by whom to them was given
 The key that shuts and opens heaven,
 Our chains unbind, our loss repair,
 And grant us grace to enter there;

  4 For at thy will they preached the word
   Which cured disease, which health conferred:
   O may that healing power once more
   Our souls to grace and health restore.

On the whole, accompaniments of this nature will run best if the outer parts contrive to assume definite curves or lines (extending perhaps over one or more phrases) or if one such line remains fairly stationary for a time while the other moves obliquely. Curves moving in contrary motion, expanding and contracting, make for a feeling of unity (especially if they are generous in length), and should be sought. For the most part it is the indefinite and jagged outline—general shapelessness—that should be avoided.

When the melody is held by the tenor, the shape of that line is clearly going to have some effect on the movements of the outer parts, and it is largely this characteristic of the triple strand of interest (i.e., melody, and two outer parts) which makes the form a little difficult to manage.

In the case of the bass-melody, the difficulty lies in a certain stubbornness which arises from two causes:

 i The shape of the bass is beyond the range of choice—except the choice of rejection.

 ii The accompanist's vocabulary is slightly reduced by the breakdown of the ever-helpful 5–6 formula. We are happy so long as we can work with figures like:

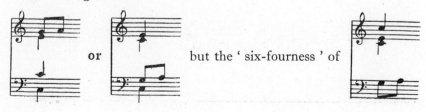

but the ' six-fourness ' of

will not satisfy. The situation can be faced, though with increased movement, by

which is manageable while it is in three parts, but becomes less satisfactory in four:

Thus there is at least a reduction in the material available. The weak six-four over a passing note, on the other hand, is very unobjectionable, and may well be allowed. The choice may rightly rest between

These slight difficulties have been mentioned with no desire to deter experiments. On the contrary, both forms of accompaniment are useful and intrinsically good, and should be persevered with.

A final reminder is given that there is no need to feel chained to one formula of accompaniment right to the bitter end:

E. H. No. 125

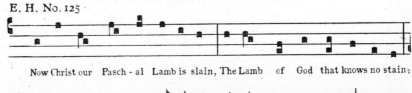

Now Christ our Pasch - al Lamb is slain, The Lamb   of   God that knows no stain;

The true O - bla - tion of - fered here, Our own un - lea - vened Bread sin - cere.

5. REGISTRATION.

Both in texture and volume the accompaniment should be distinctly light. Organs and buildings differ so vastly that it is obviously unprofitable to dogmatize, but from the nature of the harmonizations set forth in all the foregoing examples, it will be evident that very little in the way of weight or bulk of volume is anticipated.

A heavy use of the organ, besides being entirely unsuitable, inevitably tends to exert a millstone-like influence in weighing down the free movement of the voices, and producing a ponderous stiffness where an almost fairy lightness should rather be.

Restraint need not mean dullness. Variety of volume within the softer registers and contrast in colour and in pitch will afford ample opportunity for redeeming a quiet accompaniment from the dreariness which is rather depressingly implied by the word ' unobtrusive '.

A Swell diapason effect alternating with a soft 8-ft. Choir or a light 4-ft. flute on the Great, coupled perhaps to the Swell, will usually form a suitable sort of general accompaniment—homely white walls, as it were, capable of catching up and enhancing the incidental colour to which they form a background.

The 16-ft. pedal should be used sparingly. There is little room for a pedal Open Diapason, and it is a good plan to draw the Bourdon just when it is required, and otherwise to keep it off, especially if it has a tendency to ' boom '. A double on the Swell, combined or not with soft 8 ft. work, is often very useful played an octave higher.

Make use of single stops and do not always couple the Swell to the Great. An uncoupled Stopped Diapason which is not woolly may have a liquid welling quality which forms an ideal accompaniment for boys' voices; for the same purpose almost any string tone is most useful if it is not strident.

An Oboe is best in its tenor ranges, and chords there are quietly effective for supporting men's voices, especially if not drawn on too frequently. In the same locality, a quiet Clarinet may be used, though hardly for chords. On the other hand, men may be quite pleasantly accompanied by a light ' four-foot ' flue effect on the Swell standing quite clear of the voices. Conversely, boys' voices may sometimes be allowed to stand clear above rather low-set 8-ft. chords.

Chanters are best left with very light support and occasionally they may be left entirely alone, e.g., for an odd verse or so in the procession ' Hail thee, fe tival day '.

There is little or no opportunity for the flare of a full Swell, though it might perhaps be drawn on for a specially broad closing phrase such as the end of the Creed or *Gloria*, when even an Open Diapason on the pedals might be allowed to come into its own.

It is fairly safe to say that there will be practically no occasion for using the open flue work on the Great, unless perhaps for a little soloing an octave down to anchor the voices if they have a tendency to sharpen.

On the whole, the requirements of plainsong, so far as registration is concerned, may be summed up in the qualities of simplicity and resourcefulness, to which may be added a leaning towards the ' plain ', a genius for quiet variety, and a sense of balance.

No attempt has been made to tabulate a complete guide to the possibilities of suitable registration. Each player will naturally know best what the quieter beauties of his own organ may be.

CHAPTER V

THE ACCOMPANIMENT (*continued*)

Further considerations: (1) Tonality, (2) Harmony, (3) Rhythm.
1. Tonality : modal accompaniment.
2. Harmony:
   (*a*) Fifths and octaves.
   (*b*) Sixths.
   (*c*) Discords, strong and weak.
   Strong: Suspensions.   Weak: Passing Notes.
              Appoggiaturas.   Changing Notes.
                                                Discords generally.

3. Rhythm:
   (*a*) Harmonic means of marking a strong note.
   (*b*) Changes of chord at weak notes.

1. MODAL ACCOMPANIMENT.

The line along which it was argued that the matter of the accompaniment should be native of the mode may be logically produced further. Within any mode, certain notes have a prominence either of importance or of occurrence, or both, and those which pre-eminently answer this description are the final and the dominant (the anchor and the pivot). It is reasonable to require that in selecting chords with which to accompany any given melody, preference should on the whole be given to the common chords of these two notes. No difficulty, of course, will be found in using them freely; effort should rather be directed at excluding a too frequent use of some other chord or chords at their expense. It is possible to formulate rules based on a mathematical analysis which might assist an even more exacting discrimination, but it is believed that the penalty of anything like a rigid application would be the checking of spontaneity and the cramping of that flowing movement of parts which is of the very essence of a satisfying accompaniment. A watch, however, may very well be kept (particularly in any form of psalm accompaniment) that undue prominence is not given to the common chord on the dominant of the relative plagal or authentic mode as the case may be. For instance, in mode i, it is not difficult to allow the following sort of accompaniment to become the normal:

1.4

Innocent in itself, a disproportionate use of it suggests the flavour of mode ij. The risk will be found greatest in modes i, iij, and v, for reasons which will not be hard to find if reference is made to the mode table on p. 22.

Another feature which should on the whole be avoided is the modern dominant-tonic cadence. A measure of prohibition hardly seems called for, though it would be a healthy discipline to refuse its use so long as anything else was reasonably available. The material at hand is surprisingly abundant, and beautiful.

Is it ever permissible to step outside the mode? By accident, never. Promiscuous wandering is, of course, entirely indefensible, but there are one or two occasions when the deliberate transgression is at least arguable. One such is the *tierce de picardie* which is applicable to final cadences of those modes of which the third degree above the final is minor (i.e., modes i–iv), and of which the final would therefore normally be accompanied by the minor common chord thereon. Whether this chord is to be made major or not must remain a matter of taste. If the player wishes to be strict, the answer will be ' no '; yet one point at least is worth consideration, and the answer may be ' yes ' as applied to one pair of modes, and ' no ' to the other.

In the case of modes i and ij, the major third above the final is the F sharp of the mode—the ' next thing ' to the B flat in the way of accidentals; less foreign, that is, than the C sharp for instance. With iij and iv, on the other hand, the major third above the final is the G sharp of the mode—an emphatically foreign element. The fact remains that the *tierce de picardie* ending as applied to modes i and ij often has an effect of healthy beauty:

E. H. 17

Thou in man's flesh be-cam'st a child.

whereas a corresponding application in the other two modes frequently gives a quasi-modern touch of chromaticism:

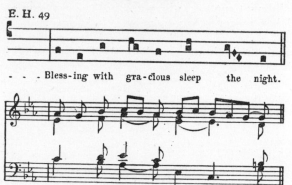

The use of the major cadence is, of course, capable of a wider application, and whether such instances as the following are to be accepted or rejected may be left for the individual's experience to decide:

In its defence it may be said that the nature of the cadence could never be mistaken. It is evidently deliberate. In any case, however, far from its being undertaken as a duty, its use should be occasional rather than regular. The beginner had better leave it alone.

The modal argument produced in favour of the accidental cadence in mode i raises a further question. If it was sometimes the custom deliberately to transpose a melody in order to gain the effect of an occasional F sharp or an E flat (see p. 27), is the use of such an accidental rigidly to be denied the accompanist? The answer seems to be that if such a liberty is taken, it must be with eyes wide open, and for a fleeting touch only. There are occasions when the casual F sharp would be ruin to the tonality; for instance, in the fourth mode, where the F natural, standing as it does only a semitone above the final, is so strikingly characteristic of the mode.[1] Where the effect of an F sharp is deliberately imported into the melody by means of transposition, it is an entirely different matter; otherwise the F sharp in mode iv should be shunned like poison. Once admitted, it is surprisingly difficult to eradicate.

In the seventh mode, however, where the F is a less critical note, an occasional F sharp introduced for the definite purpose of avoiding the tritone, or for a *tierce de picardie* cadence, does not seem to be objectionable. One or two instances have been included in the tone table at the end of this book, where at the pitch of the example the F sharp of the mode is represented by C sharp. It is easy to reject them if desired.

Again, in the sixth mode, where the B was habitually flattened, an occasional E flat will at least be characteristic of the old tonality as a whole, and may be gently condoned as an over-enthusiastic reaction from the tyranny of the leading note rising to the tonic. It is easy to re-establish the true tonality almost immediately.

Venite   vj

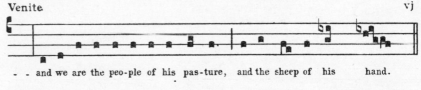

- - and we are the peo-ple of his pas-ture, and the sheep of his   hand.

However, the position of the purist who objects is theoretically unassailable, and it is undoubtedly a sterling rule to stick to the notes of the mode.

With regard to the use of the optional B flat, it is unnecessary to lay down any rules. It is available whenever required, and the accompanist's ears must tell him how it is best employed. Care must be taken not to acquiesce in a perpetual B flat, especially in modes i, ij, and vj. The B is, of course, the pure tonality, and it must be seen to that the note is not obliterated; whenever it may be used, it should be preferred. It is a great pity to throw away its bitter-sweet effect in modes i or vj. Tallis certainly knew better in his Dorian services. As an example of mode vj

---

[1] Look, for instance, at the psalm tone ending in the Asperges (*Introits*, p. 1) and substitute F sharp for the F in the centre of the neum over the word 'good-' or '-fen-'. It will at once be realised how utterly the character of the melody becomes changed.

take E.H. No. 165. The true key signature is one flat only, and the working may be in some such manner as this:

E. H. 165   vj

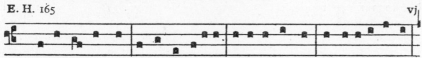

Fa-ther, we praise thee, now the night is o-ver, Act-ive and watchful, stand we all be-fore thee;

Sing-ing we of - fer prayer and med - i - ta - tion : Thus we a - dore thee.

which may be compared with the following, where the B natural of the mode is lost:

2 HARMONY. *(a) Fifths and Octaves*

' Don't be pedantic. e.g., consecutive fifths were used for centuries before a more modern technique forbade them. They can be used effectively in accompanying plainsong. The same may be said of octaves.'[1] But clearly they are to be definitely chosen: they are not to appear as the unbidden visitor. A still more modern technique welcomes them, in varying degrees and in differing circumstances according to the particular exponent, yet the harmony book remains to be written which will tell us *when* we may use them.

There seems to be something like a common consent to the cadential use of consecutive fifths rising step-wise to a major common chord, and instances have been included in examples on pp. 56, 66, and 67.

This cadence sometimes has a particularly satisfying effect where the melody has been groping around within a restricted compass just before settling down to its close:

Introit, Corpus Christi   ij

In all these instances, the fifths have been combined with consecutive octaves, and it is interesting to note that while this combination is satisfactory when the harmony is in close position, it is better to arrange the parts so as to omit the octaves if the harmony is a little more open, e.g.:

Ps. 69   i.4.

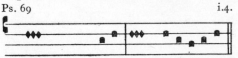

11. I put on sackcloth al-so ; and they jested upon me.

is better than

---

[1] *Church Music*, by A. S. Duncan-Jones (Robert Scott), to which attention is drawn.

An occasional touch of the octave effect produced by doubling the melody is sometimes pleasant, e.g., in the Rosy Sequence:

E. H. 238

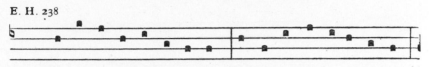

4. Je - su, thou sweetness pure and blest, Truth's Fountain, Light of souls dist - rest,

Sur-pass-ing all that heart re-quires, Ex-ceed-ing all that soul de-sires.

(b) Sixths.

Parallel sixths, of course, cause no difficulties, and in theory they may stream on at pleasure, yet in their very facileness there may lurk a danger. There is in the chord of the sixth a certain character of weakness or instability as compared with the common chord in its original position, and although, quite rightly, it will be used freely, an undue reliance on its employment may rob an accompaniment of virility. The pliancy of the material makes possible a peculiar form of accompaniment which can run about in parallel sixths with the melody, note for note, over a more or less sustained bass, especially where the melody moves stepwise. A comparatively easy form to work, it has its attractions, though it lacks the dynamic vigour of its antithesis—two parts taking the same passing notes by contrary and stepwise movement.

The two forms may be set out for comparison as follows:

Lord, have mer - cy up - on us,

As a type, the latter is almost always to be preferred as being more in character with the style of the music and the general principles of its accompaniment. Each shows the use of the pedal or organ point, but the same preference holds good in the case of the shorter standing bass, and also applies to a similar treatment of consecutive thirds:

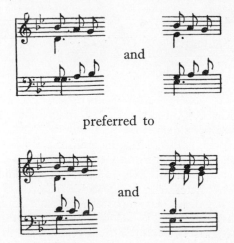

and

preferred to

and

On the other hand, it is a form which cannot be forbidden and occasional touches of it may be found acceptable. It is probably best

reserved for use in conjunction with the melody being held by a part
other than the soprano, e.g.:]

Incidentally it will be found that in this manner of working, the strong
$\frac{6}{4}$ chord seems to claim recognition more naturally, as also some minor
irregularities:

Chief-ly him the war - rior   Pri-mate of ce - les - tial chiv - al - ry &c.

In passing it may be observed that the above remarks are not directed against the idea of successive chords of the sixth which do not move about note for note with the melody. They may, of course, be used most satisfactorily either in conjunction with or apart from the organ point—or even with a double pedal, e.g.:

Ps. 36   iij. 5

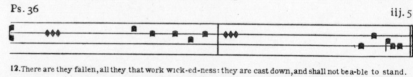

12. There are they fallen, all they that work wick-ed-ness: they are cast down, and shall not be a-ble to stand.

or the opening of the second working of E.H. 176 on p. 61.

(c) *Discords: Suspensions.*

It has been required that these accented discords should be properly prepared, i.e., that the process of suspending should consist of three successive stages:

(A) The preparation—the note about to be suspended appearing as a concord.

(B) The actual suspension as a discord over the new bass.

(C) The resolution—the suspended note resolving one degree downwards to form a concord.

The suspension may be interrupted by a weak note interpolated between (A) and (B), which is either (i) a harmony note:

or (ii) a note one degree above or below.

An extended form of this will be seen in the closing chords of the example on p. 63.

The resolution also may be interrupted or ornamented by a weak note which is an element of the chord of resolution[1]:

---

[1] Otherwise, the suspension resolving upwards is not often suitable.

or, in an extended form:

The following example shows the interrupted suspension and the ornamented resolution both employed in one neum:

As the essence of the preparation consists of an appearance of the note about to be suspended *as a concord*, its appearance as a discord is irregular. However, the following workings need not be disallowed, and the process may be known as an unprepared suspension:

Appoggiaturas.

Of the analysis of the suspension on p. 74 the elements B and C occurring without A are termed an appoggiatura—in essence, the chord at C ornamented by a discordant leaning note one degree removed.

It is sometimes referred to as an unprepared suspension, though as the element of preparation is entirely absent and the note is therefore not ' held over ', the description would seem to be a misnomer, arising, no doubt, from the similarity of effect caused by the strong discord resolving by a downward step.

It is available for use in plainsong accompaniment, though it is recommended that its employment should be exceptional. In any event, the sharpness of the discord seems to need some mitigating introduction. In the case of the suspension this is provided by the preparation (even when interrupted), which wards off, as it were, the baldness of the bare discord. Some corresponding ' protection ' seems called for here, and is best secured by using the appoggiatura only when it is approached stepwise, thus:

The third instance may be classified as an accented passing note. In each case, it will be observed, the ' protection ' consists of a note which is a factor of the chord of resolution, i.e., it is an anticipatory. The above examples may be compared with:

where the nakedness of the discord is plainly felt;

and this again may be contrasted with the following:

where the discord is a properly
prepared suspension; and

where the preparation is complete
but interrupted.

It is, of course, understood that the appoggiatura form is available only as applied to chords which are in themselves permissible. That is to say, the resolutions must be common chords or first inversions thereof.

Passing Notes.

A passing note has hitherto been treated strictly in the sense of a weak discord forming an intermediate step between two harmony notes a third apart—or two such might occur consecutively as steps between two harmony notes a fourth apart. When two harmony notes, however, are only one step apart, the latter being lower, a passing note may be intercepted a second above the former and leap down a third to the latter.

E. H. 94

The Cross shines forth in mys-tic glow.

This figure is of common occurrence, and it is useful to remember that the highest note may be thus treated. If, however, a change of chord is made at the third note, it should also be remembered that the passing note must be anticipatory, as illustrated at p. 41, thus:

Or again—

not

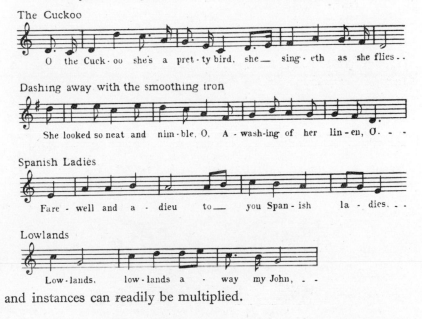

This figure also is commonly met, and affords another example of a passing note quitted by a leap. It is also interesting as being peculiarly characteristic of essentially unisonous music, and it will be recognized as a constantly recurring element in English folk-song:

and instances can readily be multiplied.

Usually there is no difficulty in treating the centre note as a harmony note, and on the whole this is the most satisfactory way, though there is no objection to treating it as a non-harmonic passing note.

It may be seen combined with its upward counterpart in the beautiful introit form of psalm tone ending for mode viij, which might be harmonized thus:

Introit psalm, Dedication Festival   ij

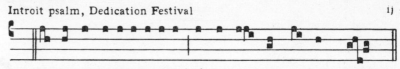

. . : the Lord hath put on his ap-pa-rel, and gird - ed him - self with strength.

though the treatment of the upward figure leaves something to be desired.

If, however, a change of chord is made at the third note of the figure, the passing note, being quitted by a leap, must be anticipatory:

Gloria V

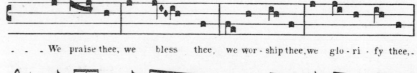

. . . We praise thee, we   bless   thee, we wor - ship thee, we glo - ri - fy thee, .

This sort of treatment will be found useful for cadences, and in such a position may be rounded off by a passing note in one of the under parts, especially if the melody-passing-note is lengthened, as it is in psalm tone i.8.

Or, greatly daring, one might sharpen the final chord, so giving a vigorous false relation.

This does not seriously affect the anticipatory character of the passing note in the melody.

Two particular figures under this heading have been dealt with in some detail because they are of such frequent occurrence, but the idea of a free passing note rising stepwise and quitted by a leap may be applied more widely.

For instance, in the All Saints Sequence (E.H. 253):

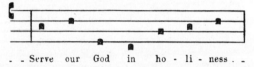

the second note might perhaps be treated as a free passing note thus:

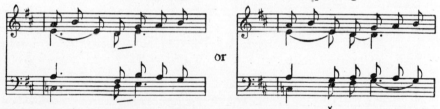

In the second example the incomplete chord at × implies the anticipatory B. This may be compared with:

which is hardly a satisfactory working, as the fresh chord (even though the bass remains unchanged) is not anticipated by the free B.

On the whole, however, the simplest and most straightforward schemes for dealing with such figures are the most satisfactory, for instance:

G

where the B forms a harmony note in each case.

In all such cases it is sufficient to remember that if a fresh chord immediately follows the discordant passing note, it should contain as one of its elements the passing note just quitted.

It may now be appreciated why in earlier stages (p. 42) attention was focussed upon the actual passage from chord to chord, and why weak discords were less jealously watched within the duration of a chord than in the act of passing to a fresh one.

Changing notes.

The following figures[1] occur fairly frequently in the more ornate forms of plainchant:

and the inner two notes in each case are capable of being handled as changing notes, i.e., as unessential (though not necessarily both as discords) while the outer two stand as harmony notes, e.g.,

More often, however, the accentuation of the neum, or the immediate context, will suggest a different treatment, e.g.:

---

[1] The changing-note figure may be regarded as an extension of the auxiliary-note

figure 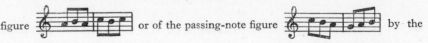 or of the passing-note figure by the

interception of a note between the second and last notes, but on the 'other side', and one degree removed from what will then be the fourth note, so as to *change* the direction of approaching this last note.

Introit, Trinity ix

Introit, Whitsunday

In the following introit for Christmas Day, the figure occurs three times, but for various reasons it has twice been preferred not to treat it as an occasion for changing-notes. At the second occurrence ('be') the treatment is a very straightforward harmonization which, however, may fall within the changing-note category, in that the fourth note is a harmony note which does not stand above a change of bass.

Introit, Christmas Day

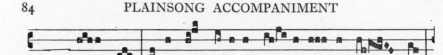

gi - ven : and the gov-ernment shall be up - on his   shoul - der :

and his Name shall be   call - ed, An-gel of migh - ty   Coun sel.

On the whole, a harmonization of this figure which involves two successive discords, the second of which coincides with a secondary stress (as usually it does), will not be welcome.

Discords in General.

The accompanist need not be at pains to analyse the nature of discords which arise from the occurrence of passing notes, auxiliary notes, pedals, etc. Chords of the seventh may be formed, yet a little discretion may be exercised in passing to a fresh chord by such a progression as:

which sometimes gives a suggestion of slipshod modernity. Usually the discord is better dispensed with by rearranging the first chord.

Beyond this, and a recollection that the tritone interval between melody and bass is best avoided (see p. 43), it does not seem necessary to formulate restrictions. Ears rather than rules should be relied on for rejecting what is unpleasant. It is sufficient to remember that the roughness of a discord may often be got round by a process of elimination (see p. 41), e.g.:

which in its turn suggests a revision of the original harmony:

Similarly, a harshly discordant effect caused by a passing note may often be mitigated by rearranging the parts so as to drive apart the notes forming the discord. This is particularly notable when the discord is that of a minor second, which may be considerably softened if it is presented as a minor ninth. Thus, in the progression:

the minor second between the treble F and the alto E causes an awkward roughness which is felt less acutely if a redisposition of parts allows the F and the E to be separated by the interval of a minor ninth, i.e., between treble and tenor, thus:

3. RHYTHM.

(a) *Harmonic Means of marking a Strong Note.*

The ordinary manner by which the accompaniment reflects the rhythm of the melody is by change of chord at accented notes. It is useful to take into account that:

(i) A change of chord may be effected by movement in an inner part without involving a change of bass:

i. Introit ending 4.

- -:world with-out end.　A - men.

Introit, Trin. xxiij

- - - . thoughts　　of peace,

(ii) Akin to this is the suspension of an inner part, for the same purpose:

Kyrie II

Lord, have mer-cy up - on　us : and in-cline our hearts to keep this law.

(iii) A change of position within a chord may be made with the same object.

(iv) Similarly, the leap of an octave:

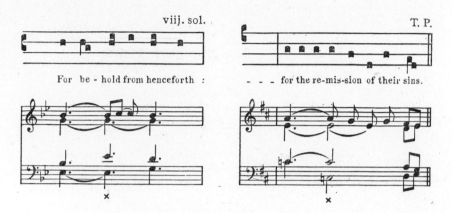

Attention may here be drawn once again to the ever-patient formula:

which is capable of bearing a stress, if required, at any point of its composition:

(b) Change of Chord at Weak Notes.

If in accompanying plainsong there is one rule which might be called cardinal, it is that which designates strong notes as the occasions for change of chord. It is even more vital than insistence on modal accompaniment. The order of importance is, first ' where ', then ' with what '.

Nevertheless, so long as the cardinal principle is firmly grasped, it is not for one moment suggested that a weak note must *never* be accompanied by a fresh chord. It will be found that, provided the movement of parts is kept slight (e.g., see p. 50), an occasional change of this sort will not really disturb the true rhythm of the text. On the contrary, an easy flowing harmony will be less prejudicial than one which is uncomfortably forced to conform with a sealed pattern.

Many instances may be found in the various foregoing examples, but a couple of workings for *Vexilla Regis* (E.H. 94) are given to serve as additional illustration:

4. O Tree of beauty, Tree of light!
   O Tree with royal purple dight!
   Elect on whose triumphant breast
   Those holy limbs should find their rest:

5. On whose dear arms, so widely flung,
   The weight of this world's ransom hung:
   The price of humankind to pay,
   And spoil the spoiler of his prey.

Occasionally such a change may be positively valuable for giving a sense of relief from a too rigidly mechanical application of the rule, especially in syllabic forms where the rhythm tends to tread regularly:

The Rosy Sequence E. H. 238

2. No word is sung more sweet than this;   No name is heard more full of bliss;

No thought brings sweeter comfort nigh, Than Je - sus Son of God most high.

A fresh chord at a weak note may even be used strategically as a corrective. For instance, there is an almost incurable tendency to maltreat the rhythm of psalm tone vj as follows:

An odd verse or two accompanied in some such way as this:

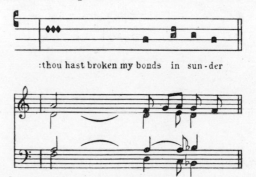

:thou hast broken my bonds in sun-der

will have a steadying effect, and intrinsically is not unpleasant.

Three points may usefully be borne in mind:

(i) An isolated change of chord is more conspicuous than one in conjunction with another fresh chord.

(ii) There are degrees of verbal weakness, and in making a choice, a change would naturally be preferred at the less weak.

(iii) A change at one of two successive weak notes is generally better at the second than at the first, e.g.:

Dedication Sequence (p. 142)

- - - Ma-ker of hea-ven and earth. .   - - - Like an ar-my splendid and ter-ri-ble. .

Far more subtle than a procession of alternating strong and weak syllables, the rhythm of the words is an evasive enough thing to catch and analyse, and the difficulty is enormously increased when it is enshrined within a melody which may have its own rhythmic contribution to add. It is not surprising that in the process of applying an accompaniment, the function of which is to reflect the one and to take account of the other, a rather more flexible handling is called for than a merely mathematical application of rules. In the very nature of things, no more than any other art can the accompaniment of plainchant be compassed by the manipulation of unqualified formulae. At least a sense of balance and proportion must be brought to bear if the whole creation is to carry the stamp of the craftsman.

CHAPTER VI

PSALMODY

Preparatory.

As the psalm-tone belongs to the simplest of all forms of plainsong—a monotone interrupted by inflexions—and as it is quite likely that the psalms may be the point where plainsong is most urgently needed, psalmody might have been expected to receive first treatment in order of time, and the accompaniment of plainsong in general to succeed at a later stage. The subject of accompaniment, however, must be treated as a whole, and although the church musician may perforce have to tackle psalms as his immediate and main objective, he must by no means feel himself excused from mastering the contents of any of the preceding chapters. At the very least the first three chapters stand as a prelude to the consideration of any accompaniment whatever, and then, if circumstances are very pressing, a study of Chapter IV may run concurrently with work at the pages which here follow. That there may be some such necessity for an early embarkation on the psalter has been kept in view, particularly by the provision of the tone-table at pp. 145–170. It would, however, have been obviously impracticable as well as undesirable to have made the present chapter a complete and self-contained guide to psalm accompaniment.

Actually the psalm-tones raise no separate problem of accompaniment and they call for no different treatment from any other form of plainsong, except to the extent to which the particular form naturally falls into its two component elements of long stretches of monotone, and variable inflexions rounding them off; and whereas the latter are always associated with some degree of rallentando, and a slightly higher proportion of chords to melody notes may therefore be expected, the monotone sections call for no change of chord at all. Although it is obviously not improper to make a change of chord at some verbal stress during a very long reciting note, yet on the whole it is better in ordinary circumstances to make no such change. Frequent movement of the bass during a monotone tends to make for a feeling of restlessness.

Apart from these points, all the ordinary principles of plainsong accompaniment apply.

Quite simply, the order of instruction will be:

1 To learn how to sing the psalms.

2 To learn some of the harmonies provided in the tone-table, and apply them.

With regard to the former stage, the first step will be to procure a thoroughly reliable psalter, and for this purpose it is assumed that the student is in possession of one of the following, irrespective of the particular psalter which may be used in his church:

The Sarum Psalter (Rev. Dr Palmer)—St Mary's Convent, Wantage.

A Manual of Plainsong (*New* Edition: Briggs & Frere)—Novello.

The Plainsong Evensong Psalter & Canticles (Hughes & Goldsmith)—Faith Press.

The Plainchant Evening Psalter and Canticles (Burgess)—Novello.

The difference between these is mainly in scope, the method of chanting being broadly identical[1].

It will be found that:

1 The music of the chant consists of eight tones, corresponding with the eight modes (with the Irregular or Peregrine tone as an addition).

2 That portion of the melody which applies to the first half of each verse (i.e., up to the colon) is invariable *for the tone*.

3 Variety within the tone is obtained by the use of different endings, which are applicable to the *second* half of each verse; and so we speak, for instance, of ' first tone, fourth ending ', or more simply ' one-four ' (i.4.), ' seventh tone, third ending ' (' seven-three ', vij.3.) and so on.

Instructions for the application of these tones will naturally be found in the introductory pages of the psalter chosen, and these must be thoroughly digested, so that the student may make the singing of any psalm a matter of perfect ease. Emphasis has already been laid on the necessity for a vocal approach to the subject, and the point is here stressed again. There is no other road whatever to psalm accompaniment, and the task must quite definitely be undertaken, audibly.

A start had better be made with a strictly syllabic ending, say i.4. for Ps. 73, viij.2. for Ps. 3, and then an ending containing a neum may be taken in hand, e.g., i.1. or i.3. for Ps. 1 and so on.

---

[1] *The Sarum Psalter* enables *any* psalm to be sung to *any* tone—an essential requirement in a community quire for instance, or in any other place where the antiphons proper to the seasons are used and the psalm tone has to be selected according to the mode of the particular antiphon of the occasion. The book is no less useful in the ordinary parish church, and it is furnished with an invaluable introduction, a mastery of which is a sufficient equipment to deal readily with any psalter. Its latest edition includes in its tone-table certain additional tone endings drawn from English sources outside the Sarum Tonale. The numerical system of pointing is an apparent rather than a real difficulty.

In *A Manual of Plainsong* each psalm is pointed for a selected tone. The principles of chanting are practically identical with those of the *Sarum Psalter*, and as the book enjoys a wide popularity, it is used as a basis of any examples which follow. An edition is obtainable with the tones done out note for note over every syllable throughout the psalter, but the organist will find it easier to use the smaller edition, memorizing the required tone (a matter of extreme simplicity), and so leaving his eye free to deal with a piece of literature rather than busying it with fitting notes to words. The system of pointing is very easy. The tones are those of the Sarum Tonale.

The Plainsong Evening Psalter is equally easy for chanting, and agrees closely with *Sarum Psalter* principles, but is pointed for selected tones only (which are indicated in modern notation over each psalm). The tones are from the Sarum Tonale with English additions, but the book contains only the psalms (and canticles) for evensong according to the Prayer-book scheme for recitation. Its usefulness is therefore restricted to churches where the psalms at Mattins are not sung and where the revised lectionary scheme of special Sunday psalms has not been adopted. This latter point may affect any psalter pointed for selected tones.

The Plainchant Evening Psalter covers a similarly limited ground. It is pre-eminently legible, and has all strong verbal accents marked so—an undeniable aid to choir-boys, and hardly less needed sometimes by their elders. Tones are drawn from slightly wider sources.

The student who has been lucky enough to have made his first intelligent acquaintance with plainsong by hearing a competent choir sing psalms unaccompanied cannot have failed to be most forcibly impressed by two outstanding characteristics in the manner of performance. One is the pause of silence at the colon marking the half-verse—long enough, it has been suggested, mentally to repeat the words ' deep breath '— and secondly, the combined diminuendo and rallentando immediately before the colon (sometimes quite slight) and similarly at the end of the verse—that ' dying down ' or ' lifting off ' which is of the very spirit of the chant. These two points, also the slight stress at the first note of a neum, and, above all, the even recitation of good reading which leaves unchecked the natural verbal rhythm of the prose, must always be kept before one in the early stages of learning to chant. They will speedily become automatic, and they naturally have a direct bearing upon the manner of accompaniment.

Having made i.4. his own as applied to Ps. 73 so that he can sing the psalm through in the proper manner with ease, the player is ready to embark upon the stage of adding an accompaniment. The simple and direct manner (for the novice at any rate) is humbly to learn by heart, say, half-a-dozen of the harmonies[1] set out in the tone-table, and then to experiment in fitting them to the words.

In using the tone-table he will observe that the harmonies suggested are clearly not all designed to fit one sealed pattern of rhythm. Just as in Ps. 73 the accentuation of verse 4, for instance, differs from that of 5, so the respective accompaniments should differ if they are going to reflect the verbal rhythm. The following accompaniments are obviously unsatisfactory:

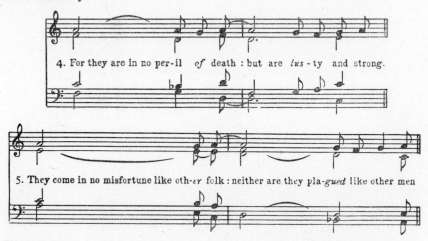

4. For they are in no per-il *of* death : but are *lus*-ty and strong.

5. They come in no misfortune like oth-*er* folk : neither are they pla-*gued* like other men

---

[1] As far as the melodies are concerned, the difficulty of learning the ' mere handful ' of psalm tones which forms the whole stock-in-trade is negligible. It inevitably solves itself in practice.

while a discriminating selection of harmonies or a slight adaptation will
result in something more appropriate, e.g.:

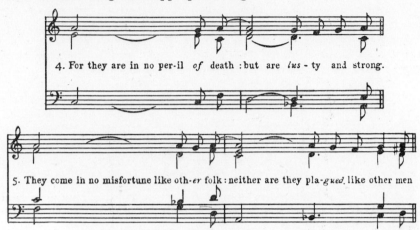

4. For they are in no per-il *of* death : but are *lus*- ty and strong.

5. They come in no misfortune like oth-*er* folk : neither are they pla-*gued*, like other men

With practice, the faculty will quite soon develop for adapting accompaniments to fit the particular rhythm, and coincidently the ability also
to make original harmonies which will satisfy the principles of proper
accompaniment. It is not claimed, of course, that the harmonies
suggested in the tone-table (pp. 152–170) are in the least degree ex-
haustive.

Special attention may here be drawn to the circumstance of a strong
verbal accent immediately preceding the first note of the mediation or
ending which itself opens with a weak syllable, e.g.:

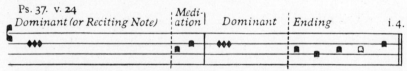

Ps. 37. v. 24

Dominant (or Reciting Note) | Medi-ation | Dominant | Ending   i. 4.

Though he fall, he shall not be càst *a*-way : for the Lord uphòld-*eth* him with his hand.

Accompaniment and verbal rhythm will clearly be at cross purposes if
the first change of chord in each half verse is made at ' a-' and ' -eth'
respectively. The change must be made in each case at the preceding
syllable instead:

. . . .cast *a*-way :   .. up-hòld-*eth* him with his hand.

This feature is so commonly met, particularly where the mediation or ending opens one degree lower than the dominant (e.g., Tones i, iv, vj, and endings of ij and viij), that it may be advisable to mark such accents whenever they occur, in order to catch the eye. In this connexion the suspension, the 6–5 formula (p. 48), or the ' contrary motion ' figures (as above at '-holdeth him '—see p. 87) are most useful. The great thing to be avoided is the *isolated* change at the weak inflexion, e.g.:

..:for the Lord up-hòld-*eth* him . . .

On the other hand, the situation may be dealt with by making no change of chord at all, either at the accented syllable or at the weak syllable which follows it.

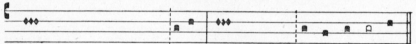

Though he fall, he shall not be càst *a*-way: for the Lord uphòld-*eth* him with his hand.

The change must thus be at the verbal stress or not at all.

The field for applying or adapting the given harmonies to the words of the psalms is now limited only by the extent of the psalter and the number of endings in the tone-table, and the player's proficiency should increase in direct relation to the amount of time he is willing to devote to chanting and work at the piano.

Before leaving him at this stage it may be well to clear away a difficulty which in reality does not exist, but the ghost of which has been known to dog the beginner's footsteps, i.e., the ' redundant note ' or extra note inserted wherever, according to the pointing, mediations or endings are made to contain a greater number of syllables than there are notes (or neums) to go round. It will, of course, be necessary for the organist to know how to *sing* it--and in this there is no difficulty, as in psalters based on selected tones, its presence and identity are clearly marked by a ⌢, while in the *Sarum Psalter* it is regulated by a few simple examples —but it is entirely unnecessary to regard it as requiring accompaniment.

The following pair of examples will illustrate the point. In the first there is a redundant note; in the second there is none:

That is to say, the harmony may remain unchanged whether there is a redundant note or no. In fact, so far as the accompaniment is concerned it does not matter *what* the redundant is; it might equally well be A or B, or even C. It is always light, and apart from the fact that it may take a shade longer to play ' e-qui-' than ' Sy-', it is the concern of the voices only. The harmony is independent of it.

The only possible exception is in the mediation of Tone iij, where an additional note is sometimes comparatively strong and may admit special treatment, e.g.:

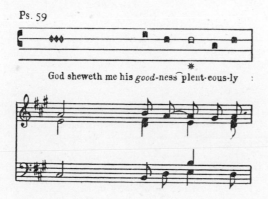

The converse of the redundant note is that very characteristic feature of the psalm-tone—the omission of a note or even a section of notes in order to fit verbal requirements. Thus, the abbreviated or abrupt form of mediation is constantly occurring, e.g.:

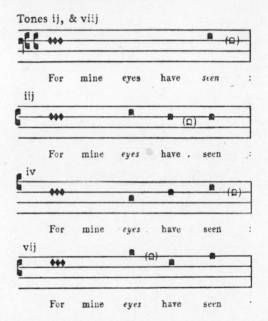

Tones ij, & viij

For   mine   eyes   have   *seen*   :

iij

For   mine   *eyes*   have .   seen   :

iv

For   mine   *eyes*   have   seen   :

vij

For   mine   *eyes*   have   seen   ·

and its treatment is so obvious as to call for no further comment[1]. More serious omissions, such as the entire absence of a reciting note in short verses, are no more difficult to deal with, but may well be specially marked in the psalter so that the player is not caught unawares.

It need hardly be pointed out that this capacity for ' short cuts ' is a mark of the psalm-tone's naturally elastic vitality, and one of its glories.

AT THE ORGAN.

Lay-out. It is not within the scope of these pages to enter into the history of the different methods of singing the psalms in the Christian Church from the earliest days. For information of this nature the reader is

---

[1] The reason for admitting this apparent complication is the concern of the compiler of the psalter rather than of the organist. The fact emerges that there is such a thing as a purely musical accent proper to the chant, and it is a function of the pointing to arrange that, where it exists, it shall coincide with a verbal stress. (It does not exist in the mediations of i and vj, hence there is no abrupt mediation here). This is simple in the case of mediations, but in endings also there is a musical accent (quite apart from accents proper to neums, as such), and examples may be found where the pointing cannot arrange a coincidence of stress. In such cases the musical accent gives place to the verbal, e.g., the musical accent in the ending iv.4 is the penultimate note; see, however, Ps. 94, v.21. But once again, it is the psalter which arranges this. The player's duty is to see that violence is not done to the verbal rhythm put before him.

referred to the chapter on Psalmody by Rev. Dr G. H. Palmer in *Elements of Plainsong*. It is sufficient to say that, although there is evidence of psalms having been sung ' full ' throughout, or by a solo voice, the Gregorian psalm-tones as they have come down to us are inextricably associated with the idea of alternating contrast in some form or other, and the tradition as we have received it calls for the treatment of alternate verses in contrast either of volume or of pitch[1]—this quite independently of the use or disuse of the liturgical antiphon. The particular method most commonly employed of securing this alternation is by contrasting either men's voices with boys' (or women's), verse by verse, or by similarly interchanging one or two voices (' chanters '— generally men) with the full choir (and congregation). Aesthetically, as well as traditionally, the value of this constant interplay of light and shade is immense.

The exact manner of working will be as follows:

The organ gives out the notes of the intonation by way of introduction, for the purpose of establishing pitch and tonality; thus, for example:

For verse i, the first half is sung by one or two chanters and the second half is sung full. The remainder of the psalm is sung in the following manner, according to the method adopted:

	METHOD 1.	METHOD 2.
Verse 2	Chanters	Boys
Verse 3	Full	Men
Verse 4	Chanters	Boys
Verse 5	Full	Men
	&c.	&c.

An alternative way of dealing with the first verse according to Method 2 is for the chanters to sing the verse throughout.

Gloria is treated in precisely the same way as the ordinary psalm verses, i.e., in strict rotation just as it happens to fall, and the intonation should not be used. That has fulfilled its duty when the chanters have sung it at verse i. Hence, if a second psalm follows immediately with the same

---

[1] It should be stated, however, that in convent quires, the alternating verses are commonly sung ' side after side '.

tone, the first verse of the new psalm is started straight away without intonation. In such circumstances that verse is sung full throughout, i.e., it is not ' chanted '. The *Amen* of *Gloria* is usually sung full.

Registration. The general remarks at p. 63 seem to call for no particular modification as applied to the accompaniment of psalms. As alternate verses are opposed either in volume or pitch, the obvious scheme will be to rely on a sort of dual foundation consisting of a couple of suitably quiet combinations prepared on different manuals, and to use these more or less alternately, modifying them by addition or subtraction just as the need for variety is felt. If a third manual is available, it will, of course, be welcomed for use as occasion may admit.

As an instance, supposing the method of singing is ' chanters and full ', quite a manageable sort of scheme might be to draw a light 8-ft. stop or combination on the Swell, and a Stopped Diapason and light 4-ft. Flute on the Great, which may be coupled to the Swell. The pedal had better be coupled to Swell only, not to the Great, and a quiet pedal Bourdon might be drawn, though this should be given a rest frequently; 16-ft. pedal, as a habit, should be guarded against.

The first half verse will be chanted, unaccompanied. For the second half (full), the Great and pedals would be used. Verse 2 would be accompanied on the Swell without pedal, and during its course the Great Stopped Diapason might be put in. The resulting combination will probably be found a very suitable ' average ' sort of support for full verses, especially if the Flute is quietly bright with no fiery quality. (It may here be well to add that a judgement of quality should be made in conjunction with the voices, not in the empty church where, if the organ is well placed and the building resonant, the Flute may sound alarmingly bright). Modifications may now be made at will, by exchanging the 4-ft. Flute for the Stopped Diapason; by putting in the pedal Bourdon for a couple of ' full ' verses; by drawing a Principal on the Swell, opening the box, and using the Swell only for a full verse; by reducing the Swell and accompanying the chanters an octave higher; by getting rid of everything on the Swell except an Oboe, and accompanying the chanters by a few lowish chords on it; and so on almost without limit. If a choir manual is available perhaps a 4-ft. Harmonic Flute will serve a turn played an octave lower, or a Gamba combined with a quiet 2-ft. stop may be useful for a ' full ' verse, especially if chords are played ' round the melody '. The *Amen* concluding the psalm will need a little breadth and the original Great combination will probably be in request again, with pedals.

Plenty of variety with very modest means has here been suggested. Let it not be thought, however, that a restless striving for variety should be aimed at. Far better that the accompanist should devote his entire attention to a right clothing of the rhythm of the chant with simple harmonies, and stick almost for ever to a couple of stock combinations, than that he should disturb the repose and tranquillity of the rhythmic flow by stop-handle gymnastics. It will only be when his accompaniment has become really spontaneous that he will be able to bother his head much about variety of registration.

The Colon. The pause here must be jealously guarded; there is a tendency for it to disappear altogether, but it should be retained even if the psalms are being said, without music. The singers' part here is silence, but a combined silencing of voices and organ may be rather too abrupt to be pleasant, and in full verses the player had better tide over the pause by transferring the last chord of the mediation to the Swell with his left hand as soon as the voices have attacked the last note, holding it there till the second half is reopened on the Great; or more simply by holding over, on whatever manual is being used, just one note or a portion of the chord which closes the mediation. If a soft swell is being used (e.g., for chanters), the whole chord may simply be held over; or, on the other hand, silence might not be too pronounced here.

Whereas there is a distinct pause at the half verses, there should be no break whatever between verse and verse, or verse and *Gloria*.

Endings and Finals. Psalm-tone endings do not always end on the final of the mode, for the reason that, according to the original scheme of things, the psalm tone always led on immediately into the antiphon, and it was not necessarily until the end of the latter that the mode's final was reached. But the whole unit of antiphon, psalm, and antiphon did end on the final. As the corresponding unit is now more usually the psalm alone, it seems desirable to achieve finality by some means or other. Where the ending closes on the final, it is naturally the chord of the final that will be used to complete the *Amen*, and the same chord may frequently be made to do the same service if the last note happens to be a component part of that chord, e.g.:

(The final of the fifth mode, as here transposed, is D.)

If, however, this cannot be done, some sort of bridge may be constructed by improvising for a couple of bars or so, to flow quite naturally to the proper final of the mode, for instance:

Such additions will naturally be modal, simple, and short, and an endeavour should be made to keep up some sort of free rhythmic feeling; a procession of solid chords will hardly be suitable. Perhaps it may be added that if the player is not handy at making a satisfactory improvisation spontaneously, he had better work a few out on paper beforehand, or quite frankly let the matter rest without an attempt to reach the final. He might certainly do worse, and there are arguments on his side. For instance, if the singing is unaccompanied, what of the final? Clearly the voices cannot wander off in quest of one: conditions must be accepted just as they are. It is at least arguable that it is no duty of the organ to provide a kind of dummy antiphon.

No addition will, of course, be called for if the psalm leads straight on to another one sung to the same tone.

Solemn modulations. These decorated forms of the psalm tone are reserved, so far as the choir offices are concerned, as a mark of honour for the gospel canticles of *Benedictus* at Mattins and *Magnificat* at Evensong. They call for no specially detailed instructions beyond those given in the psalter. It may be noted that inasmuch as the long reciting note is interrupted in its course by the addition of ornaments, and is further decorated in the first half of each verse by an ornamental use of the intonation, the form approximates more closely to the less severely simple kinds of plainsong.

With regard to the pace at which these solemn modulations should be sung, a custom has arisen of taking them deliberately slower than the simple forms. There appears, however, to be no very compelling reason why solemn *Magnificat*, for instance, should be sung at a slower pace than any other plainchant. It seems at least as reasonable to ask those concerned to regulate the accompanying ceremonial of censing, as to drag out the proper music or to eke it out with interludes. The function of *Magnificat* is not, surely, to serve as a musical accessory to the censing.

The solemn modulations are not applied to *Nunc Dimittis* nor should the intonation be used as a decorative feature at the beginning of each verse. This canticle is treated as a psalm.

Miscellaneous points.

(i) The use of plain octaves as an accompaniment is too often over-looked. Reserved for an occasional verse or half-verse, it forms, indeed, an effective and refreshing contrast. It is best suited to simpler endings and larger volumes of tone; it would not be preferred, for instance, in accompanying boys' or chanters' verses.

(ii) The essential function of the intonation is to form a bridge between the final note of the antiphon and the reciting note of the the psalm into which it leads. Seen in this light, it is a matter of little consequence that the intonations of different tones are sometimes identical. In the absence of the antiphon, however, the practical use of the intonation becomes changed. It cannot always be a final guide to tonality, and in the event of consecutive psalms having different tones with identical intonations (e.g., iij and viij), it will reduce the risk of confusion if the organist emphasizes the changed tonality by transposing the second psalm a semitone down or up.

(iii) Although the structure of the normal psalm verse consists of a sequence of dominant, mediation, dominant, and ending, it is a mistake to let each element harden into a kind of water-tight compartment. Even beyond the special consideration of a verbal stress immediately preceding the mediation or ending (p. 95) the first note of these elements should not be regarded as an invariable signal for a change of bass.

(iv) Neither is it essential to mark every new verse or half-verse by a change of chord. On the contrary, if opportunities occur of allowing verse to flow naturally into verse, or mediation into second half, without interruption, they should be seized from time to time.

Experience will prove that a regard for such points as the last two mentioned will not only make for a feeling of unity, but will definitely contribute to that unhasting, unruffled character which marks an adequate accompaniment of the psalm tones.

*   *   *   *

Having put the hand to the plough, is there not sometimes the temptation to look back? The restraint of the mode—for so it must seem in the beginning—the almost childlike simplicity of harmony, the undrawn reserves of instrumental power, the leaning to an unemotional interpretion, the ' free verbal rhythm pressing through a quickly flowing melody ',—are not these things very new? Are we really called to such revolution? Let us draw inspiration from the great and ever youthful Elizabethan divine who, though he may not have been contemplating the identical form as we have learnt it, faces the same problems, and links hands with us across the ages to St Basil, bearing witness that the ideals which we have set before us are no mere revival of an antique fashion, still less the shibboleth of a moment, but that they are fundamentally the unique method of answering questions and fulfilling desires which are rightly uttered now, and have been so uttered throughout the Christian ages.

' In Church music curiosity and ostentation of art, wanton or light or unsuitable harmony, such as only pleaseth the ear, and doth not naturally serve to the very kind and degree of those impressions, which the matter that goeth with it leaveth or is apt to leave in men's minds, doth rather blemish and disgrace that we do than add either beauty or furtherance unto it. On the other side, these faults prevented, the force and equity of the thing itself, when it drowneth not utterly but fitly suiteth with matter altogether sounding to the praise of God, is in truth most admirable, and doth much edify if not the understanding, because it teacheth not, yet surely the affection, because therein it worketh much. They must have hearts very dry and tough, from whom the melody of psalms doth not sometime draw that wherein a mind religiously affected delighteth. Be it as Rabanus Maurus observeth, that at the first the Church in this exercise was more simple and plain than we are, that their singing was little more than only a melodious kind of pronunciation, that the custom which we now use was not instituted so much for their cause which are spiritual, as to the end that into grosser and heavier minds, whom bare words do not easily move, the sweetness of melody might make some entrance for good things. St Basil himself acknowledging as much, did not think that from such inventions the least jot of estimation and credit thereby should be derogated: 'For' (saith he) 'whereas the Holy Spirit saw that mankind is unto virtue hardly drawn, and that righteousness is the less accounted of by reason of the proneness of our affections to that which delighteth; it pleased the wisdom of the same Spirit to borrow from melody that pleasure, which mingled with heavenly mysteries, causeth the smoothness and softness of that which toucheth the ear, to convey as it were by stealth the treasure of good things into man's mind. To this purpose were those harmonious tunes of psalms devised for us, that they which are either in years but young, or touching perfection of virtue as not yet grown to ripeness, might when they think they sing, learn. O the wise conceit of that heavenly Teacher, which hath by his skill, found out a way, that doing those things wherein we delight, we may also learn that whereby we profit!' [1]

---

[1] Richard Hooker, *Laws of Ecclesiastical Polity*, Book V, 38. (1597).

EXAMPLES

Asperges me

Thou shalt purge me, O Lord, with hys-sop, and I shall be clean: Thou shalt wash me, and I shall be whi-ter

than snow. *Ps.* Have mercy up-on me, O God: af-ter thy great goodness. Thou shalt purge me, O Lord, with

hyssop, and I shall be clean: Thou shalt wash me, and I shall be whi-ter than snow. *v.* And according to the

multitude of thy mercies: do a-way mine of-fen-ces. Thou shalt purge &c. Glo-ry be.. Ho-ly Ghost. As it was...

(Antiphon repeated)

and ev-er shall be: world with-out end. A-men. Thou shalt wash me, and I shall be whi-ter than snow.

Introit—Ascension Day   *Viri Galilei*

Ye men of Gal-i-lee, why stand ye gaz-ing up in-to hea-ven? al - le - lu-ya :

in like man-ner as ye have seen him go-ing up in-to hea-ven, so shall he come a-gain, al-le - lu - ya,

al - le - lu-ya, al - le - lu-ya *Ps.* And while they looked stedfastly toward heaven, as he went up:

be-hold, two men stood by them in white ap - pa - rel : which said un - to them.

Ye men..&c. Glo-ry be.. As it was..ev-er shall be : world with-out end. A - men. Ye men..&c.

(Antiphon repeated)   (Antiphon repeated
                                                        if there is time)

Introit—Whitsun Day   *Spiritus Domini*

The Spi-rit of the Lord hath fill-ed the whole world al - le - lu-ya

and that, which con - tain - eth all things hath know - ledge of the voice,

al - le - lu - ya al - le - lu - ya al - le - lu - ya.

Introit—Trinity xxij   *Si iniquitates*   iij

If thou, O Lord, wilt be ex-treme to mark in-i - qui - ties, Lord who may a - bide it?

for un-to thee be-long-eth mer - cy, O God of _____ Is - ra - el.

110

Kyrie VII. Orbis factor

Kyrie V. —*Lux et origo*

1, 2, 3.

Lord, have mer - - - - cy.
Ky - ri - e e - - - - ley - son.

4, 5, 6.

Christ, have mer - - - - - cy.
Chri - ste e - - ley - son.

7, 8.

Lord, have mer - - - - cy.
Ky - ri - e e - - ley - son.

9.

Lord, have mer - - - - - - cy.
Ky - ri - e e - - ley - son.

Creed

I believe in one God, the Fa-ther Al-migh-ty, Ma-ker of hea-ven and earth,

and of all things vi-si-ble and in-vi-si-ble. And in one Lord Je-sus Christ,

the on-ly be-got-ten Son of God. Be-got-ten of his Fa-ther be-fore all worlds.

God of God, Light of Light, ve-ry God of ve-ry God. Be-got-ten not made, be-ing of one

substance with the Fa-ther: by whom all things were made. Who for us men, and for our sal-va-tion

113

114

Sanctus III

Ho - ly, Ho - ly, Ho - ly, Lord God of hosts. Hea-ven and earth

are full of thy glo-ry. Glo - ry be to thee, O Lord most high.

A - men. Bless-ed is he that com-eth in the Name of the Lord.

Ho - - san - na in the high - - est.

or

116

Sanctus X

Ho-ly, Ho-ly, Ho-ly, Lord God of hosts. Heaven and earth are full of thy glo-ry. Glo-ry be to thee, O

Lord most high. A-men. Bless-ed is he that com-eth in the Name of the Lord. Ho-san-na in the high-est.

Agnus Dei III

O Lamb of God, that ta-kest a-way the sins of the world, have mer-cy up-on us

O Lamb of God, that ta-kest a-way the sins of the world, have mer-cy up-on us

O Lamb of God, that ta-kest a-way the sins of the world, grant us thy peace.

Agnus Dei X

O Lamb of God, that ta-kest a-way the sins of the world, (✠) have mer-cy up-on us. *ij At Requiems* (✦) grant them rest.

O Lamb of God, that ta-kest a-way the sins of the world, (✠) grant us thy peace. *cnd* (✦) grant them rest ev-erlasting.

Gloria in excelsis V

(G.S.)

Glo-ry be to God on high. And in earth peace, good-will to-wards men. We praise thee. We bless thee.

We wor-ship thee. We glo-ri-fy thee. We give thanks to thee for thy great glo-ry. O Lord God, heavenly

King, God the Fa - ther Al - migh - ty. O Lord, the on - ly be - got - ten Son,

Je - - su Christ. O Lord God, Lamb of God, Son of the Fa - ther.

That ta - kest a - way the sins of the world, have mer - cy up - on us.

Thou that ta - kest a - way the sins of the world, have mer - cy up - on us.

Thou that ta - kest a - way the sins of the world, re - ceive our pray - er.

Thou that sit - test at the right hand of God the Fa - ther, have mer - cy up - on us.

For thou on - ly art ho - ly Thou on - ly art the Lord. Thou on - ly, O Christ,

with the Ho - ly Ghost, art most high In the glo - ry of God the Fa - ther. A - - men.

Gloria VI

Glo-ry be to God on high. And in earth peace, good-will to-wards men. We praise thee. We bless thee.

We wor-ship thee. We glo-ri-fy thee. We give thanks to thee for thy great glo-ry. O Lord God, hea-ven-

-ly King, God the Fa-ther Al-migh-ty. O Lord, the on-ly be-got-ten Son, Je-su Christ. O Lord God,

Lamb of God, Son of the Fa-ther. That ta-kest a-way the sins of the world, have mer-cy up-on us.

Thou that ta-kest a-way the sins of the world, have mer-cy up-on us. Thou that ta-kest a-way the sins of the world,

re-ceive our pray-er. Thou that sit-test at the right hand of God the Fa-ther, have mer-cy up-on us.

For thou on-ly art ho-ly Thou on-ly art the Lord. Thou on-ly, O Christ, with the Ho-ly

Ghost, art most high In the glo-ry of God the Fa-ther. A-men.

Venite
Men (M) and Boys (B), or Chanters (C) and Full (F) vj

O come, let us sing un-to the Lord: let us hear-ti-ly re-joice in the strength of our sal-va-tion:

let us come be-fore his pre-sence with thanks-giv-ing, and shew our-selves glad in him with psalms.

122

For the Lord is a great God, and a great King a-bove all gods: in his hand are all the cor-ners of the earth,

and the strength of the hills is his al - so. The sea is his, and he made it: and his hands pre-par-ed

the dry land: O come, let us wor-ship, and fall down, and kneel be-fore the Lord our Ma-ker:

for he is the Lord our God, and we are the peo-ple of his pas-ture, and the sheep of his hand. To-day, if

ye will hear his voice, hard-en not your hearts: as in the pro-vo-ca-tion, and as in the day of temp-ta-tion

124

Psalm* 110, iij. 2

126

Psalm 5. i.4. *(Chanters & Full)*

Pon-der my words, O Lord : consider my *me*-di-ta-tion. 2 O hearken thou unto the voice

of my calling, my King and *my* God : for unto thèe *will* I make my prayer. 3 My voice

shalt thou hear be-times, O Lord : early in the morning will I direct my prayer unto

thee, *and* will look up. 4 For thou art the God that hast no pleasure in wick- *ed* - ness :

neither shall any *e*-vil dwell with thee. 5 Such as be foolish shall not stand in *thy* sight :

for thou hatest all them *that* work van-i-ty. 6 Thou shalt destroy them that speak

leas -ing : the Lord will abhor both the blood -thirs -ty *and* de -ceit -ful man.

7 But as for me, I will come into thine house, even upon the multitude of thy *mer* -cy :

and in thy fear will I worship toward thy *ho* - ly tem - ple. 8 Lead me, O Lord,

in thy righteousness, be -cause of mine èn - *e* - mies : make thy way *plain* before my face.

9 For there is no faith -fulness in *his* mouth : their inward parts are *ve* -ry wick -ed - ness.

10 Their throat is an o -pen sè - *pul* -chre : they *flat* -ter with their tongue.

11 Destroy thou them, O God; let them perish through their own i -ma -gi - *na* -tions :

cast them out in the multitude of their ungodliness, for they have re-bèl-*led* a-

Sw. *p*

-gainst thee. 12 And let all them that put their trust in thee *re*-joice: they shall ever

be giving of thanks, because thou defendest them; they that love thy Name shall be

joy-ful in thee. 13 For thou, Lord, wilt give thy blessing un-to the *righ*-teous:

and with thy favourable kindness wilt thou de-fènd *him* as with a shield.

Glory be to the Fa-ther, and to *the* Son : and *to* the ho-ly Ghost. As it was in

the beginning, is now, and ev-er *shall* be : world with-*out* end. A-men

Antiphon upon the psalms at Compline

Have mer - cy * up-on me, O Lord, and heark-en un - to my prayer. o i ou e a e

Antiphon upon Nunc dimittis at Compline

Pre - serve us * O Lord while wa-king, and guard us while sleep - ing :

that a-wake we may be with Christ, and a-sleep may rest in peace. o i ou e a e

Antiphon upon the first psalm at Lauds of Septuagesima Sunday

Have mer - cy, O God, up - on me, * and cleanse me from my wick - ed - ness :

for a - gainst thee on - ly have I sinn - ed. o i ou e a e

Magnificat, *vj. Solemn modulations* *

My soul *doth* mäg-ni-fy the Lörd : and my spï-rit hath rejoiced in *God* my Sa-viour.

2 --For *hë* häth re-gärd-ëd : the löw-liness of *his* händ-maid-en. 3--For *bë*-höld from hënce-förth :

all generä-tions shall *call* mïe bless-ed. 4 For hë that is mighty *häth* mäg-ni-fi-ëd mïe :

and ho-*ly* ïs his Name. 5 And hïs mercy is *ön* thëm that fëar him : throughout all *gen*-ër-a-tions.

6 He häth shew-*ëd* strëngth with his arm : he hath scät-ter-ed the proud in the imaginà-*tion*

* *The occurrence of a neum is marked by two dots over the syllable concerned. Syllables covered by the intonation are underlined*

N.B. The harmonies suggested in the Tone Table under ij.1. might be used en bloc for Nunc dimittis

E.H. 49

To opposite page

iv

E. H. 51

To opposite page

Aeterna Christi munera

If the hymn is treated thus in the manner of pure plainsong, (as it well may be), it will be necessary to revise the Amen so as to bring it into conformity with the true mode, thus:—

Easter Procession
Salve, festa dies

E. H. 624

Hail thee, Festival Day! blest day that art hallowed for ever;

Day wherein God o'er-came hell, and arose from the dead.

2 Lo, the fair beauty of earth, from the death of the winter arising,

Every good gift of the year now with its Master returns.

(continued overleaf)

Chorus

To opposite page

Hail thee, Fes - ti - val Day! blest day that art hal - lowed for ev - er; -

Chanters

To opposite page

(Or an octave lower)

3. He who was nailed to the Cross is__ God and the Ru - ler of all things;

4. God of all pi - ty and power, let thy word be as - sured to the doubt - ing;

Day where-in God o'er - came hell, and a - rose from the dead.

All things cre - a - ted on earth wor-ship the Ma - ker of all.

Light on the third day re - turns: rise, son of God from the tomb!

*Or 6-5 over B♭, if preferred.

Easter Sequence (E.H. 130)

First boy

5 The Tomb of Christ, who is liv-ing, The glo-ry of Je-su's Re-sur-rec-tion :

Second boy

6 Bright an-gels at-test-ing, The shroud and nap-kin rest-ing.

Third boy

7 Yea, Christ my hope is a-ris-en : To Ga-li-lee he goes be-fore you,

Men

8 Hap-py they who hear the wit-ness, Ma-ry's word be-liev-ing A-bove the tales of Jew-ry de-ceiv-ing.

Full

9 Christ in-deed from death is ris-en, our new life ob-tain-ing. Have mer-cy, vic-tor King, ev-er reign-ing!

Dedication Sequence (E. H. 172)

To opposite page

Si - on's daughters! Sons of Je - ru - sa - lem! All ye hosts of hea - ven - ly chi - val - ry!

v. 1.
5.
9.

v. 2. Christ our Sa-viour weds on this fest - i - val   Ho - ly Church the Pat-tern of Righteousness,
6.

Now the Bride re - ceiv - eth his be - ni - son, Tast - eth now the joys of the Pa - ra - clete,

v. 3.
7.

v. 4. Mo-ther meet for sin-ful hu - ma - ni - ty,   Life's sure ha - ven, rest for the sor-row-ful,
8.

(Another melody)

Lift your voi - ces, sing - ing right mer - ri - ly Al - le - lu - ya.

Whom from depths of ut - ter - most mis - e - ry He hath res - cued

Kings and Queens with ju - bi - lant me - lo - dy Call her bless - ed.

Strong pro - tect - ress, born in a mys - te - ry Ev - er won - drous.

THE
TONE-TABLE

SUGGESTED HARMONIES FOR ACCOMPANYING THE PSALM-TONES COMMON TO THE *MANUAL OF PLAINSONG* AND THE *SARUM PSALTER*

THE TONES OF THE PSALMS

TONE I

For the Solemn Modulations of Benedictus *and* Magnificat,
see p. 168

TONE II

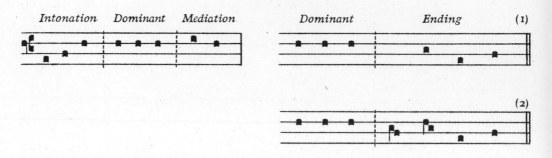

For the Solemn Modulations of Benedictus *and* Magnificat,
see p.169

TONE III

The same for
Canticles

TONE IV

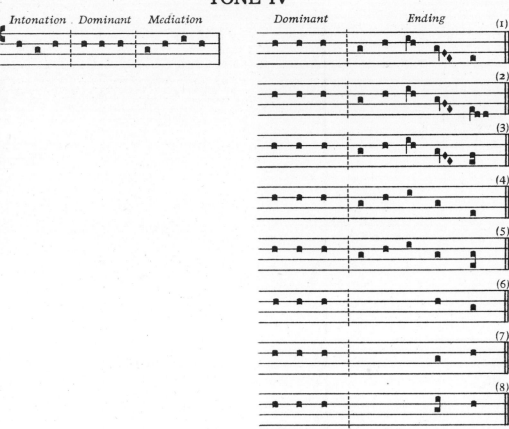

For the Solemn Modulations of Benedictus and Magnificat, see p.170

TONE V

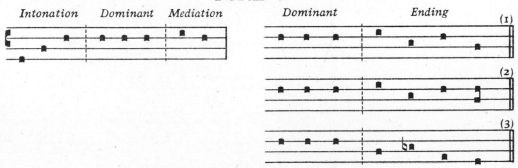

TONE VI

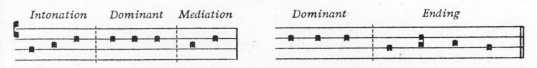

For the Solemn Modulations of Benedictus and Magnificat, see p.168

150

TONE VII

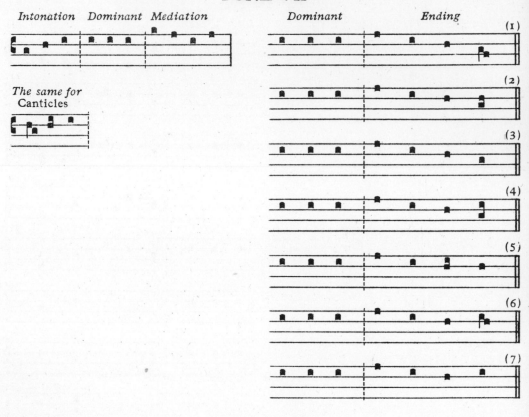

TONE VIII

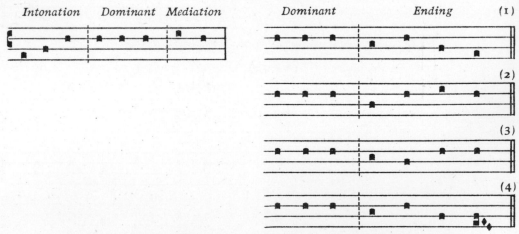

For the Solemn Modulations of Benedictus *and* Magnificat, *see p.169*

The Irregular or *Peregrine* Tone

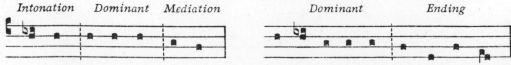

NOTE

1. The enclosing of a note or sign within round brackets ( ) indicates an optional use; the omission of notes thus enclosed will involve a proportionate lengthening of the note preceding the bracket.

2. Notes within square brackets [ ] are for use, or not, according to the requirements of the pointing.

3. All the tones have been reduced to a common dominant (A). The final and dominant of the mode are indicated at the head of each page.

4. A small perpendicular line over the upper stave indicates the close of the reciting note (the dominant).

5. In the following harmonies no regard is paid to the position or identity of redundant notes (see p. 96).

152 Tone i

Tone i

154

Tone ij

(or over pedal F♯)

Tone iij

Mediation :   *Ending* __4__   **5**   **6**

Tone iv

Mediation: *Ending____* **1**   **2**   **3**

Note on Tone IV (especially iv. 4, iv 5).

The first five endings of the fourth tone consist of five notes or note-groups as compared with the more usual four or three in the other tones, and therefore afford peculiar opportunities for reflecting the various verbal accentuations which may occur within them. It therefore follows that corresponding opportunities are here offered to the organist to help out the rhythm by a discriminating accompaniment, and it has been considered advisable to draw special attention to the treatment of endings 4 and 5, which are the simplest and most commonly used.

The following combinations of accent are typical; but, though alarming in number, are capable of great simplification.

a.	1.		the	láw	that	he	gáve	them
b.	2.	punishedst	their	ów̃n	in - vén -	tions
c.	3.	footstool	for	he	is	hó -	ly
d.	4.		con - démn	the	iń - nocent	blood
	5.		to	his	ów̃n - - - -	hín - drance	(Sarum)
	6.		Lórd	our	Gód is	hó -	ly
	7.		slán - der -	ed	his	néigh -	bour
	8.		Lórd - - - -		and	he	héard	them	(Sarum)

(N.B.—The possible occurrence of a redundant syllable immediately before the final syllable calls for no observation.)

It will readily be seen that 6 and 7 are merely variants of 2 and 3 respectively by the addition of a strong syllable immediately preceding the inflexion. The treatment of this feature by the use of a suspension (or other device) will have become familiar in Tone i; however, examples are given opposite under the fifth ending.

Number 5 will be recognized as variant of 2, and 8 a variant of 7 (or 3) and call for no exceptional treatment.

Thus, in fact, the types are reduced to the first four—a, b, c, d—, the last of which, where the musical accent is displaced by a strong syllable immediately preceding it, is rarely met; and of these, b and c are often so closely akin as to call for no differentiation in treatment. Attention is drawn, for instance, to Example iv. 5, c, which by its light texture and conjunct movement is equally suitable for use with a c or b rhythm.

It is not impossible to find rhythms which do not readily sort themselves exactly under the above classes, but a mastery of the principles underlying the following examples will enable the student to treat such cases with ease, if indeed any special treatment is called for.

For beginners, a rough working rule emerges:—

Determine whether the ending begins on a strong or weak syllable, and use an a accompaniment or b/c accordingly. If b/c is immediately preceded by a strong syllable, approach the ending by a suspension or a six-to-five.

Tone iv

160

Tone iv

Tone v

*Required for the pointing of the Sarum Psalter, Plainsong Evening Psalter, and Plainchant Evening Psalter

Tone vj

Mediation: Ending

Tone vj

Tone vij

Medi-
adion: Ending___1   2   3

Tone vij

Tone viij

Tonus Peregrinus

Medi-
ation:

Ending (as in Sarum Psalter)

SOLEMN MODULATIONS

Tones i & vj

Or an octave higher

SOLEMN MODULATIONS

Tones ij & viij

* *For convenience the D♯ proper to Tone ii is omitted*

SOLEMN MODULATIONS

Tone iv

(Another ending)

INDEXES

INDEX OF SUBJECTS

INDEX OF EXAMPLES

The following melodies have been drawn on to illustrate the construction of accompaniments. Big figures indicate harmonisations of *complete* melodies. Little figures denote *fragments* of melodies. Italic figures indicate the *numbers* of hymns in *The English Hymnal*. Accompaniments of plainsong hymns in *Songs of Praise* (Oxford University Press) are indicated by the letters S.P.